JOSÉ FERNÁNDEZ

PASSION FOR BASEBALL, PASSION FOR LIFE

Mango Publishing Group
in collaboration with
the Miami Herald

HERALD
BOOKS

For permission requests, please contact the publisher at:
Mango Publishing Group
2850 Douglas Road, 3rd Floor
Coral Gables, FL 33134 USA
info@mango.bz

For special orders, quantity sales, course adoptions and corporate sales, please email the publisher at sales@mango.bz. For trade and wholesale sales, please contact Ingram Publisher Services at customer.service@ingramcontent.com or +1.800.509.4887.

Library of Congress Cataloging
Names: Spencer, Clark
Title: José Fernández / by Clark Spencer
Library of Congress Control Number: 2016917891
ISBN 9781633536142 (paperback), ISBN 9781633536135 (eBook)
BISAC Category Code: SP003000 SPORTS & RECREATION/Baseball/General

Front Cover Image: June 1, 2015 (Hector Gabino/el Nuevo Herald)

Back Cover Image: September 14, 2015. (Carle Juste/Miami Herald)

JOSÉ FERNÁNDEZ: *Passion for Baseball, Passion for Life*
ISBN: 978-1-63353-614-2

Printed in the United States of America

"I prefer not to think of this as the end of his life but the beginning of his legend."

— Jeffrey Loria, Miami Marlins team owner, September 29, 2016.

TABLE OF CONTENTS

FOREWORD

The always smiling José Fernández in his early days as the Miami Marlins pitching ace. (Miami Herald)

Clark Spencer, Miami Herald Sports Columnist

The moment he saw me enter the Marlins' clubhouse, José Fernández motioned me over to his locker. It was the middle of the afternoon on a Friday, two days before his fatal boat accident.

"I've got a story for you," he said.

Music spilled out of speakers. Players went about their routines. Hitters grabbed bats and headed to the indoor cage to work on their swings. Pitchers dawdled, gazing down at the screens on their cell phones or staring up at TVs.

It was business as usual, a typical day in the hours leading up to the game — any one of the 162 that make up a season.

"Whatcha got?" I asked him.

I had dealt with hundreds of players during my 17 seasons covering the Marlins, none quite like Fernández. He was not only richly talented, but blessed with a personality to match. He had the charisma of Dontrelle Willis and cockiness of Josh Beckett, all wrapped into one 24-year-old package.

Fernández was at ease talking with most anyone, and that included sportswriters, even ones — such as myself — more than twice his age. He and I weren't friends away from the ballpark. We never socialized.

But from the time the Marlins drafted him in 2011, we had maintained a professional relationship, one without conflict despite the us-vs.-them mentality that often develops between players and the reporters who cover them. He was a player who didn't mind engaging in small talk. He was "accessible," meaning he didn't make himself scarce when there was something we wanted to ask.

And, save for one memorable instance when he was hiding the severity of the injury that resulted in Tommy John surgery, he was always honest.

"They've drug-tested me twice in three days!" Fernández exclaimed with incredulousness. "You mean to tell me they can't get it right the first time, have to do it twice? What's that about?"

As part of Major League Baseball's drug program designed to weed out cheats, the testers were working the Marlins' clubhouse that week, collecting urine samples from randomly selected players. All players are tested at some point, often multiple times during the year.

Fernández wasn't opposed to testing. Not at all. But twice in three days?

Finally, he rolled his eyes, shook his head, and smiled the way only he could.

"Look, they can test me all they want," he continued. "I can pee all day long. I'll never run out of that."

Fernández always seemed to find the humor in any situation, which was part of his appeal.

He brought a killer's instinct to the mound. He was highly competitive. He yearned to win. But Fernández did it in a way that was unlike others, with a Little Leaguer's enthusiasm that never waned from his first day in the majors to his last.

"When I think about José ... I see such a little boy in him," Manager Don Mattingly said through sobs the morning after the boating accident. "That's the joy that José played with and the passion he felt about playing."

His drive and unbridled passion — so rare among pro athletes who oftentimes appear stone-faced, almost morose — was genuine. It was so atypical that it was often misread and could rub others, namely opponents, the wrong way.

When Fernández hit his first big-league home run toward the end of his rookie season in 2013, it incited a benches-clearing brouhaha. A lot of it had to do with the added flair Fernández gave to it, flipping his bat, admiring the shot, and taking his sweet time rounding the bases.

It infuriated the Atlanta Braves, most of all Chris Johnson, then their third baseman. Johnson stormed toward home plate, confronting Fernández in a finger-pointing outburst. But after Johnson joined the Marlins this season, his opinion of Fernández changed.

"I had one view of him," Johnson said of his opinion of Fernández in that moment, "and it was completely wrong. The number one reason why it pissed me off is because he was so good. I'm grinding. I'm trying to get a hit as hard as I can, and he's out there having a good time, smiling, laughing, doing whatever he wants on the baseball field."

That was always him.

Fernández came along at the perfect time, a time when the Marlins and their fans needed him most.

The Marlins were coming off a dud of a first season in their new ballpark. The 2012 team had been such a monumental bust that management wasted little time in tearing up the roster, trading off its priciest players in a salary dump that infuriated its small fan base. What remained on paper was a 2013 team that stood zero chance of success.

With just one minor-league season under his belt, Fernández was invited to major league spring training camp in 2013. He arrived with no expectations of actually making the Marlins' Opening Day roster.

"I don't want to go crazy thinking about where I'm going to be, what I'm going to do and where I'm going to go," Fernández said at the time. "I just want to go out there every fifth day, pitch, and help my team win."

But Fernández made clear he had high aspirations.

"I want to be the best," Fernández said. "I'm not going to lie. I don't want to be second best. I want to be the best."

To no one's surprise, Fernández was ultimately sent to the minors that spring with the belief that, after a bit more seasoning, the Marlins would call him up later in the season, perhaps as early as June.

That was the plan.

But on the eve of Opening Day in New York, the Marlins dropped a bombshell. We were summoned to manager Mike Redmond's office, where then president of baseball operations Larry Beinfest announced that not one – but two – of the team's starting pitchers were injured and unable to start the season in the rotation.

Who would replace them?

"Get ready," Beinfest said. "José Fernández. THE José Fernández."

The headline that ran with my story: "In shocker, 20-year-old pitcher José Fernández makes Miami Marlins starting rotation."

Fernández , like everyone else, was caught by surprise.

"I wanted to laugh. I wanted to cry," Fernández said of his reaction when Marlins owner Jeffrey Loria broke the news to him in a phone call. "It is crazy."

Beinfest acknowledged the Marlins were taking a chance with a 20-year-old "kid," especially one with such limited minor-league experience.

"This has the potential to have some criticism, saying the guy hasn't pitched in Double A, and this and that," Beinfest said. "But if you have a special guy that's ready to do it, and he's mature mentally and physically, which we believe he is, we want him to get the experience now."

Fernández told us he was neither scared nor nervous about making his Major League debut.

"The only thing I was [ever] scared about was getting in that boat, getting shot at," Fernández said of his harrowing defection from Cuba. "After that I'm not scared about anything else. I've been in jail. I've been shot at. I've been in the water. That's why, when people say to me, 'Are you nervous, are you scared?' I'm not scared to do anything."

Fernández was an instant success, one of the few bright spots in what turned into a 100-loss season. He went 12-9 and was named Rookie of the Year.

Then came 2014 and a major setback.

Fernández's fastball velocity was down noticeably during a start in San Diego, after which he said he wasn't feeling well due to a steak he had eaten before the game.

The problem was not steak. It was his arm.

Fernández underwent Tommy John surgery and missed the next 13 months, returning midway through the 2015 season.

But in the 2016 season, he was better than ever.

José Fernández with Budweiser Clydesdales. (Clark Spencer/Miami Herald)

He made his second All-Star appearance, posted one of the highest strikeout rates in Major League history, and when we spoke to him some 12 hours before he lost his life in a boating accident along with two others, he talked of becoming even better.

Now we'll always be left to wonder.

A few days after the tragedy, I picked up my phone and began scrolling through old photos, looking for several in particular. In March, during spring training, Fernández saw the Budweiser Clydesdales positioned near the Marlins' offices. They had been brought to the ballpark to parade before fans.

He asked if I would take a picture of him with the world-famous horses. I snapped a few photos of the young pitcher in his Marlins uniform posing next to the animals before texting the pictures on to him.

When I looked at them again, noticed how closely he appeared to be studying the horses, as if they were some sort of circus animals, it struck me.

Fernández was a kid at heart.

INTRODUCTION

Thursday, September 29, 2016

HEARTBREAKING GOODBYE

What Miami has been dreading all week finally happened Thursday: the unbearable goodbye to Marlins All-Star pitcher José Fernández.

In a televised service Thursday at St. Brendan Catholic Church, just a day after thousands of mourners passed by Fernández's casket in a public ceremony, Fernández's mother, Maritza, his beloved *abuela*, Olga, girlfriend Maria Arias, a roster of former and current Marlins and scores of family and friends grieved the player killed suddenly in a violent boat crash early Sunday.

Spanning more than two hours, the service celebrated a player who at just 24 was known as much for his big personality and dramatic escape from Cuba as the fierce curve ball that made him one of baseball's best young talents.

"Every time he greeted you, that smile hit you. It was the window of his soul," his agent, Scott Boras, said in a tribute he struggled to tell through tears.

Clark Spencer, September 14, 2015. (Carl Juste/Miami Herald)

"His two most passionate places were on the water and on the mound," he said. "Both represented his rights and the freedom he most coveted. Ironically, the waters that brought José to us are the same waters that took him to a new freedom, the high heavens."

Fernández was found dead early Sunday after his 33-foot SeaVee, the *Kaught Looking*, crashed on a jetty leading into Government Cut. State wildlife officers are still investigating the crash, which also killed Eduardo Rivero, 25, and Emilio Macias, 27.

Maritza Fernández and Maria Arias after memorial service, September 29, 2016. (Roberto Koltun/el Nuevo Herald)

Fernández's mother, grandmother and girlfriend occupied the front pew in a packed sanctuary filled with the famous and not so famous, brought together by their friend's death. Singer Marc Anthony sat beside Marlins President David Samson. Behind the family were the pallbearers, some of whom made up a tight-knit group of fishing buddies dubbed JsCrew, clothed in the same black number 16 Fernández jerseys they wore during Wednesday's public ceremony.

Among the baseball greats: batting coach Barry Bonds, Hall of Famer Tony Pérez, and former Marlins pitcher Alex Fernández, who befriended the young pitcher. Shortstop Alex Gonzalez and team manager Jack McKeon, from the Marlins 2003 World Series-winning team, also attended. Washington Nationals pitcher and Hialeah native Gio Gonzalez was excused from his team's Thursday game to attend. The Marlins play them Friday.

"It's a big fraternity," Alex Fernández said before the service, confessing that the young player had left him starstruck. "Being who I am and what I did, I idolized him. That's how much respect I had for this kid."

A hearse bearing Fernández's casket arrived at St. Brendan's with a police escort about 1:20 p.m., followed by a motorcade carrying his family and nine buses bearing mourners, including Cuban reggaeton singer Alexander Delgado from Gente de Zona. Most exited with their heads bowed, black No. 16 pins on their suits.

Teammate Dee Gordon shaved No. 16 on the bottom left side of his head. Gonzalez wept on the steps of the church, next to a mound of flowers, candles and Cuban flags left behind Wednesday.

"There may be a better baseball player, but never anyone like him," said Cuban-American fan Antonio Lopez. "Only one player like him is born every century."

About 60 fans gathered outside the church, many of whom also attended Wednesday's processional from Marlins Park.

"If we knew where the cemetery was, we'd go, too," said lifelong baseball fan Perla Gonzalez, who spent three hours at the church the day before.

Fernández's mother emerged from a black car clutching a crucifix, arm in arm with the young pitcher's grandmother. His girlfriend followed. As they did Wednesday, the pallbearers once again flexed their arms in tribute.

The Reverend José Alvarez led a traditional funeral mass, in Spanish and English, searching in his sermon to comfort a family still wrestling with the unexpected death. A large portrait of a grinning Fernández stood on an easel near the altar.

"Death cannot end anything, right? Life continues up there. And the people that live in Christ in eternal life, they're busy. They are profoundly connected to those that they left behind, to those that they so generously loved," he said. As evidence, he pointed to Gordon's surprising homer at Monday's game against the Mets.

"You don't believe me? Have a conversation with Dee Gordon, right here, a skinny little guy who was not supposed to hit it that far Monday night," he said.

One of the most intimate eulogies came from Boras, the agent, who described Fernández's three greatest moments: buying a house for his mother, becoming a U.S. citizen and learning that he was going to become a father to a daughter the couple planned to name Penelope.

"He called and said, 'I bought my mother a house.' He wept. 'Can you believe it,' he said? 'I'm this little Cuban boy and I bought my mother a home in the United State of America.'"

Family and friends carry the casket of José Fernández after a memorial service at St. Brendan Catholic Church, September 29, 2016. (Roberto Koltun/el Nuevo Herald)

The father-to-be also worried about what the future held for his daughter.

"He wanted to know, am I going to be a good father? And I told him, 'You're going to be a great father because you're going to treat your child in the same way that your mother treated you and you'll know exactly what to do,'" he said. "The next day he ordered a baseball glove in all those colors he loved and he put 'Penelope' on it."

The story left Arias, Fernández's girlfriend, hunched over weeping.

Family friend and Tampa attorney Ralph Fernández said the player faced life in the same way he played baseball.

"He was not rational and prudent. He was a risk-taker, and he pushed the envelope with just about everything he did," he said. "He lived his life like he threw his fastball: hard. But he enjoyed every second of it."

Many who spoke talked of Fernández's unrestrained passion, and of beginnings, not ends, as if death were just another milestone for the All-Star. The funeral, they said, was not a farewell, but the beginning of an immortal tribute.

"He set the standard for making baseball fun," said team owner Jeffrey Loria. "He was a superstar human being. A year ago he tweeted, and you can look it up, he tweeted, 'If you were given a book with the story of your life, would you read the end?' I prefer not to think of this as the end of his life but the beginning of his legend."

As the service ended, mourners gathered near Fernández's casket, draped with a white pall embroidered with a gold cross, for a final blessing from Alvarez. The pallbearers, arms again flexed upward, loaded it into the hearse where Fernández's mother and grandmother, who on Wednesday bestowed kisses on the casket, once again seemed unable to let it go. The family did not disclose burial plans for the player's remains.

Clark Spencer,
Chabeli Herrera and
Jenny Staletovich

Chapter 1

NIGHTMARE

Investigators examine the scene of the accident that took the lives of José Fernández and two friends, September 25, 2016. (Patrick Farrell/Miami Herald)

Sunday, September 25, 2016

CATASTROPHE

Miami Marlins pitcher José Fernández, who fled Cuba on a speedboat eight years ago to become one of baseball's dominant players and a hometown hero to fans well beyond the stadium walls, died early Sunday in a violent boat crash off South Beach. He was 24.

Two friends were also killed in the accident, which remains under investigation and led Major League Baseball to promptly cancel Sunday's home game against the Atlanta Braves.

Miami Marlins fan Luis Santos, 34, wearing his José Fernández shirt, hugs his daughter, Alegna, 6, September 25, 2016. (Carl Juste/Miami Herald)

Fernández, a right-hander with a wildly precise fastball and brutal curveball, was originally scheduled to start in Sunday's game but was rescheduled for Monday's Mets game, a rare weekend day off that may have led the young pitcher to stay on the water longer.

News of the death was relayed to the Marlins when they were called about the crash Sunday morning and asked to confirm Fernández's address. Stunned teammates appeared in black jerseys at an afternoon press conference, still clearly numbed by their teammate's sudden death.

"When I think about José, I see such a little boy. The way he played, there was just joy with him," Marlins Manager Don Mattingly said, unable to continue speaking.

Late Sunday, authorities still had not confirmed the identities of the other passengers aboard the 32-foot SeaVee, named the *Kaught Looking*, but they were identified by WSVN, who talked to their families at the medical examiner's office, as Eduardo Rivero and Emilio Macias. The medical examiner posted death notices for both men on its website with no ages or other identifying information except that both died at 3:15 a.m. Sunday.

Macias' Facebook page said he worked in wealth management for Wells Fargo Advisors. Rivero's Facebook page said he worked for Carnival Corporation. Sunday evening, members of the Braddock Senior High alumni Facebook group identified the victims as former students.

Both Macias' and Rivero's families set up gofundme accounts Sunday to help pay for funeral expenses.

The Miami-Dade Police Department said one of the men is the son of a department detective but provided no other information.

Emilio Macias, left, and Eduardo Rivero are shown in photos from Facebook, undated.

The crash occurred about 3:15 a.m., so violent that the noise alerted a Miami Beach police officer on patrol who used his cellphone to call a Miami-Dade County Fire Rescue patrol boat, said Fire Rescue Captain Leonel Reyes. About the same time, a Coast Guard patrol boat returning to the Miami station also reported seeing the boat overturned on jetty rocks at Government Cut. Its navigation lights were still on, with debris in the water.

Within minutes, Miami-Dade divers were on the scene and found two bodies under the boat, submerged in water washing over the jetty, Reyes said. Divers located a third body on the ocean floor nearby about 4:15 or 4:30 a.m., he said.

Unsure if there were more victims, divers continued searching through the night and early morning. A Miami-Dade helicopter also searched from above, along with the Coast Guard boat, officials said. The search was called off about 9 a.m. after the victims' families said no other passengers were aboard. Fire Rescue then transported the bodies to a staging area at the Coast Guard station in Miami Beach, Reyes said.

Investigators said they were not sure where Fernández and his friends, dressed in T-shirts and shorts, were headed, or where they'd come from. But they say the boat was traveling south at full speed when it struck the jetty and flipped.

None of the three was wearing a life vest. Investigators do not believe alcohol or drugs played a role in the crash, but toxicology tests will be performed as part of the autopsies. Lorenzo Veloz, spokesman for the Florida Fish and Wildlife Conservation Commission, told USA Today that Fernández likely died on impact.

"It's a tragic loss for the city of Miami, for the community, for baseball, and for anyone who ever met José," said Veloz, who said he had run into Fernández on the water several times during routine safety checks.

"I'm sorry. I'm getting goosebumps right now," he said. "It's really hitting home."

The Fish and Wildlife Conservation Commission will head the investigation of the crash.

Fernández, who posted a picture of his pregnant girlfriend just five days ago, was considered one of the Marlins' biggest stars and one of the best pitchers in baseball. He was the team's first-round draft pick in 2011 and the National League rookie of the year in 2013. He was finishing up his finest season in the majors, and expected to make his final start of the season Monday after his appearance Sunday was pushed back.

His death hit teammates hard and triggered an outpouring of grief. On their way into the stadium Sunday, Marlins slugger Giancarlo Stanton and A.J. Ramos walked with their heads lowered and said nothing. Second baseman Dee Gordon openly wept. Mourning fans came to leave flowers. In New York, Cuban player Yoenis Céspedes taped up a Fernández jersey in the team's dugout.

During the press conference, Marlins President David Samson said after the team received the morning call, they struggled to come to grips with the news. Fernández's number 16 was stenciled at the mound in Marlins Park, and his number displayed prominently around the stadium.

Marlins Park, September 25, 2016. (Carl Juste/Miami Herald)

"When you talk about a tragedy like this, there are no words. There is no playbook," Samson said. "We will play tomorrow."

Politicians around Miami and the state also offered condolences to Fernández's family and vowed to celebrate his life.

"His death is a huge loss for our community," Miami Mayor Tomás Regalado said in a statement.

Athletes shared their memories as well.

"*Hermano,* wherever you are, you know how much I loved you," tweeted Yasiel Puig, who like Fernández was a Cuban athlete and one of baseball's most exciting, rising stars in recent years. "*Sin palabras.* My heart is with the families."

Stanton tweeted: "I gave him the nickname *Niño* because he was just a young boy Amongst men, yet those men could barely compete with him. He had his own level, one that was changing the game. EXTRAORDINARY as a person before the player. Yet still just a kid, who's joy lit up the stadium more than lights could."

Growing up in communist Cuba, Fernández was jailed after failing on one of several attempts to flee the nation. In a harrowing escape hard to believe even in bigger-than-life Miami, he rescued his mother in dark waters in the Gulf of Mexico after hearing someone go overboard, not realizing until he found her that it was his mother. They crossed the border from Mexico, stepping foot in Texas, on April 5, 2008. He was 15.

"I've been in jail. I've been shot at. I've been in the water," Fernández told the Miami Herald in 2013. "I'm not scared to face [New York Mets slugger] David Wright. What can he do?"

An avid boater, Fernández filled his Instagram account with pictures from the water, including shots of him holding catches including dolphin and snapper, the Miami skyline from the water and relaxing on the beach. Many reference J's Crew, a saltwater fishing team. One includes a picture of the *Kaught Looking*, with the "K" facing backward — the baseball symbol for a strike called by an ump — and lined in Marlins colors.

Veloz, the fish and game officer, said the boat was well known to authorities. Veloz said he had even stopped the boat several times with Marlins players aboard, including Fernández, to conduct safety inspections.

Still, even though it sounds like the captain of the boat had experience and navigational equipment, nighttime brings the most perils for boat operators. Hazards can be impossible to spot without the aid of a GPS device or careful attention to navigation lights designed to identify safe channels and flag obstructions.

When divers arrived early Sunday, the night was still dark and water very choppy, Reyes said. What caused the accident was unclear, he said.

José Fernández's Instagram picture of the stern of the Kaught Looking, undated.

"Even though we're not investigators, we ask ourselves the same question. These are young kids and why and how, we couldn't tell anything," he said. "They weren't dressed for partying. Just in T-shirts and shorts. They could have been just going out for a nice night and ended up in tragedy."

While darkness presents its own challenges, lights ashore cause problems, too, and interfere with night vision, Reyes said.

The brightness of South Beach at night can also obscure lights on markers and buoys that indicate safe passage, said one local rescue captain.

"When you're facing the city, those lights are very hard to discern from the street lights and car lights," said Rand Pratt, owner of the Sea Tow operation based in Key Biscayne. "It's pretty significant, especially if you're coming in from the ocean to the city."

Tides can also obscure the jetty, which at high tide can sit just inches above the water line.

"They just stick out a foot" at high tide, Reyes said. "They're very dangerous at night. The visibility is not very good."

Boaters who spoke to the Miami Herald on Sunday also said the north jetty juts out farther to the east than the south jetty, which sometimes catches boaters off-guard. The rocks farthest to the east are submerged, as well, and marked on the edge by a buoy that knowledgeable captains know will tell them if they're too far inland.

Scene of tragic boat crash

Jose Fernandez was aboard a 32-foot SeaVee that struck the north jetty at Government Cut while heading south at full speed. The boat flipped, landing on the jetty and killing Fernandez and two friends.

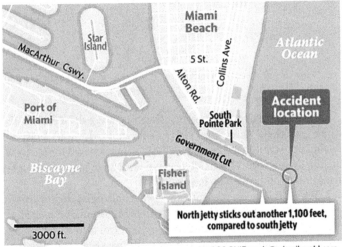

MARCO RUIZ mruiz@miamiherald.com

While none of the victims was wearing a life jacket — a practice frowned upon by safety advocates — it's also typical. "That's every boater in Miami," Reyes said.

Photos of the vessel show damage to the hull near the front of the boat, in a spot that would have been underwater during operation. Veloz said the boat is believed to have struck the jetty. But Omar Blanco, a lieutenant in the county fire department and head of its union, said it's not just the jetties that can cause boaters problems, but the submerged rocks around them.

"We've seen that happen all the time," Blanco said of boating mishaps near Government Cut. "There are rocks underwater you don't see. People run aground there."

No information on services had been released late Sunday, but the families of Macias and Rivero had started GoFundMe pages to raise funds for funeral expenses.

"It brings us great grief to announce the passing of our new beautiful angel Eduardo Rivero," his page said. "A man full of life, full of love, and full of happiness, was taken too soon with so much left to live for. Due to this tragedy we reach out to you for help as his family cannot afford funeral arrangements."

Macias' page called him "an amazing son, brother, grandson, boyfriend, cousin, friend. Due to this unexpected tragedy we reach out for help to assist our family with funeral expenses. We will forever be grateful."

By 2 p.m. Sunday, the jetty was cleared of the wreckage and a sunny day had brought out the normal crowds of beachgoers and strollers.

Towing company removes the wreckage of the *Kaught Looking* from Government Cut, north jetty accident site, September 25, 2016. (Patrick Farrell/Miami Herald)

Juan Viviescas, 16, stood alone at the end of the South Pointe pier, staring at the jetty. He wore an orange Marlins athletic shirt, and teared up as he spoke of his favorite player.

"I'm a pitcher also," said Viviescas, a junior at Mater Academy in Hialeah Gardens. "He had so much support because of how he played the game. With so much heart and intensity. Like it was his last game."

Viviescas came to South Beach with his mother and father on a Sunday that was supposed to unfold very differently. Viviescas hadn't been to a Marlins game since the summer started. "I was actually going to go today. With my parents," he said.

Clark Spencer, David J. Neal, Douglas Hanks, David Smiley,
Jenny Staletovich

Sunday, October 2, 2016

ANATOMY OF A TRAGEDY

The season was dwindling down to a few games and the Marlins were once again on the verge of going home without making the playoffs, but José Fernández was still bubbling like a Little Leaguer on Opening Day as he talked to reporters.

He was excited about pitching his next game, gushing over an upcoming family vacation in the Keys, wired about his plans to bicycle 30 miles a day over the winter. Reminded that he hadn't either pitched a complete game or hit a home run this season, he retorted with mock hauteur: "Not yet." A boundless future was always in front of Fernández.

"We have an incredible group of guys here," he said of the Marlins. "Things here and there happen, stuff happens, we know how it is. But I think we do believe in ourselves as a team."

But Fernández's future was not boundless. It would end 12 hours later on a pile of rocks in the inky predawn blackness of the sea just off South Beach, where his boat upended like a broken toy. As Fernández said, things happen, but few are as tragic and mysterious – and, possibly, needless – as the September 25 crash that ended the lives of an ebullient young rags-to-riches star and two others aboard his boat, and broke a million hearts across South Florida.

It will be months, if ever, before government investigators figure out exactly what happened out there in the dark water around the craggy stone jetty that protects Government Cut, the channel between PortMiami and the open sea.

All the known witnesses are dead. The shattered remains of Fernández's sleek, fast boat – the *Kaught Looking*, written in the Marlins' font with the K facing backwards like the ones baseball fans make on their score sheets to record a called third strike on a pitch so crafty or overpowering that a batter can't even swing at it, just watch in frustration and awe as it crosses the plate – will provide some clues. So, maybe, will the testimony of friends who saw or talked to him in his final hours. But a detailed reconstruction of those hours is full of mystifying gaps.

A night of foreboding

Practically everybody in baseball agrees that there was no more exuberant player in America than José Fernández. If he made a great play, he laughed and smiled. (There's a hugely popular video of him, a couple of years back, miraculously snatching a rocket-shot line drive out of the air over his head, robbing Colorado Rockies shortstop Troy Tulowitzki of a hit. You can easily read Tulowitzki's bewildered lips: "Did you catch that?" And Fernández's chortled reply: "Yeah, I did!") And if somebody made a great play against him, he also laughed and smiled: OK, you got me that time.

His congenital joy extended to his personal life, and why not? He escaped Cuba on a boat and arrived in Florida as a penniless 15-year-old; even when he first reported to the Marlins, he didn't have a suitcase, just a couple of shopping bags carrying everything he owned. Now he was making $2.8 million a year as one of the brightest young pitchers in the game, expected to grow to a multi-year contract worth $200 million or more when he became eligible for free agency after the 2018 season.

Certainly there was no trace of ill humor when he gave his final interview to Clark Spencer and Tim Healey, beat writers for the Miami Herald and South Florida Sun Sentinel, respectively, shortly before the Marlins played the Atlanta Braves on the night of Saturday, September 24. And he was still jovial – maybe even more so – after the Marlins won. Fernández's next pitching assignment had been unexpectedly delayed 24 hours until Monday, so he could go out after the game. He began asking friends on the team if they wanted to join him for a nighttime spin on the *Kaught Looking*.

Fernández loved the *Kaught Looking* nearly as much as he loved baseball. It was a 32-foot, open-air SeaVee powerboat that could hit 60 mph. He used it for both fishing (favorite prey: swordfish) and partying and sometimes just to pop over to the Bahamas for lunch on Cat Cay. Social media sites bristled with pictures of his boating buddies wearing T-shirts labeled J's Crew (possibly named for organizer Jessie Garcia) and rocking rods, reels and bikinis.

To many people, the idea of cruising the waters off South Beach in the wee hours of the morning sounds like a walk on the wild side. But in the nocturnal rhythms of baseball players, who don't get off work until 10:30 or 11 p.m., late-night socializing is simply a routine fact of life.

Nonetheless, Fernández couldn't find any takers for his offer that Saturday night. "That night I told him, 'Don't go out,' " recalled outfielder Marcell Ozuna, Fernández's best friend on the team. "I told him I couldn't go out that night because I had the kids and my wife waiting for me."

Miami Marlins center fielder Marcell Ozuna, June 24, 2016. (Matias J. Ocner/Miami Herald)

Instead, Fernández headed for the Cocoplum Yacht Club, where he docked his boat, while calling other friends to invite them along. And sometime after he left the Marlins clubhouse, his mood turned abruptly downward.

The first evidence showed up in texts and phone calls from one of Fernández's buddies: Eduardo Rivero, a 25-year-old executive in the sales department at Carnival Corporation. Rivero called his businessman friend Will Bernal around midnight to say he was driving over to the dock to join Fernández on the boat. The pitcher, he added, was upset after an argument with his girlfriend. Fernández "was stressed and wanted to go out," Bernal said, recalling his conversation with Rivero to the Miami Herald.

Maria Arias, sister-in-law of one of Fernández's boating buddies, had linked up with him five months earlier, after the breakup of his relationship with a former Marlins cheerleader. The 24-year-old Arias was soon pregnant. Fernández was clearly excited about the baby; a Facebook video of a party where Arias gave him a pink cake to clue him in to the gender shows him laughing with delight.

And last month he posted a picture of Arias in a bikini, baby bump clearly visible. "I'm so glad you came into my life," Fernández wrote. "I'm ready for where this journey is gonna take us together. #familyfirst"

Nonetheless, Fernández had told friends on the team that while he was pleased at the prospect of being a father, he didn't intend to be a husband any time soon. And in his final interview, when he was asked if he planned to marry during the baseball off-season, Fernández replied crisply: "No. No. No. No."

Arias hasn't talked to reporters since the accident. So what they argued about – or even if they really did argue, because no eyewitness has publicly surfaced; Bernal is merely relating what he was told – remains unknown.

Whatever the case, it sounded to Bernal like Fernández wasn't in the right frame of mind to be operating a boat in the middle of the night. Bernal, who had once been out on the ocean in the dark and found the experience alarming, tried to talk his friend out of going along.

"I did my best to convince him not to go," Bernal said. "It's just a recipe for disaster."

When Bernal's arguments didn't work, he told Rivero to at least turn on his iPhone's GPS tracker so Bernal could make sure they were OK. Their text conversation was laden with foreboding.

"Yo man please be careful bro," Bernal texted.

"I will bro," Rivero replied.

"Try to keep him close to shore if you go out," Bernal urged.

"Trust me it's not my time yet," Rivero replied.

Over the next hour, as Bernal watched television, he checked on the boat's progress through his iPhone tracker. The boat appeared to be cruising uneventfully in Biscayne Bay. But at 12:55 a.m. it stopped on the Miami River at American Social, an upscale waterfront pub that most nights is packed with Brickell's young and beautiful, choosing from an "endless selection of craft beers" while munching duck confit hash and black truffle short ribs.

American Social Bar & Kitchen, Miami, September 30, 2016. (Marsha Halper/Miami Herald)

Fernández and Rivero went into the bar, then called a close friend of Rivero's: Emilio Macias, a burly client associate at Wells Fargo Advisers who lived in the Neo Vertika luxury residential building towering above American Social.

Macias, who celebrated his 27th birthday on Friday, had turned in for the night. But Rivero urged him to come downstairs and chat with Fernández; it might be a way to recruit a lucrative new client.

So Macias threw on blue jeans and a gray Fly Emirates T-shirt, pulled a baseball cap over his head and walked out the door. He didn't plan to go out on the boat, just exchange a few words with Fernández, a man he'd met for the first time earlier that day.

But the conversation lingered. Photos of the three men at American Social were posted on various social media accounts around 2:35 a.m. A few minutes later, on an impulse, Macias jumped onto the *Kaught Looking* for what he expected to be a quick spin around Biscayne Bay.

Back at Bernal's apartment, he was no longer monitoring the boat on his phone. Convinced it was tied up safely at American Social and any danger had passed, he fell asleep around 2 a.m., shortly after sending Rivero a final note at the bar: "Wish I was with you guys. I need more guy time."

"Bro I wish," Rivero replied, and then his phone went silent.

The unkindest cut

Where the *Kaught Looking* and its impromptu crew went for the 35 minutes following their departure from American Social, and what they did, is unknown. Some answers may eventually emerge from examination of the boat's navigation equipment and the cellphones the men carried in their pockets, but if investigators have found anything, they haven't revealed it.

There's less doubt about who was piloting the boat. Though no forensic evidence has been released yet, most of his acquaintances assume Fernández was at the controls. He barely knew Macias, and Rivero's friends say he had little boating experience.

What's certain is that, at some point, the men left Biscayne Bay and headed out into the open sea beyond Miami Beach – perhaps to cruise north alongside South Beach, a boater favorite, or south toward Key Biscayne. And sometime not long after 3 a.m. they approached the granite jetties that line Government Cut, the channel that big commercial ships use to reach PortMiami.

Government Cut was opened in 1902 after the federal government literally hacked off the southern tip of Miami Beach, which became Fisher Island, to create an opening to the port on

Dodge Island. The deep channel in the cut is kept clear by the jetties.

The jetty on the north extends about 3,000 feet east into the ocean from Miami Beach; the one on the south, about 2,000 feet east from Fisher Island. The space in between them is about 900 feet wide.

A lot of boaters trying to use Government Cut to enter Biscayne Bay find it challenging. Accidents around the jetties are not uncommon, and while most of them are the seagoing equivalent of fender benders that boaters don't even bother to report, there have been at least two fatal accidents since 1984, claiming a total of five lives.

"That's a difficult jetty to navigate," said Scott Wagner, a Miami attorney who specializes in maritime law. "It's somewhat difficult even during the day. The jetty is there, blocking the way you might ordinarily come into the channel, and it's tricky. At 3 a.m., it's much worse, because of the vision problems." In the dark, the black jetties are nearly impossible to see – especially during higher tides, when they rise barely a foot above the water.

North jetty of the entrance to Government Cut, September 26, 2016. (Carl Juste/Miami Herald)

Government Cut poses fewer problems for the nighttime arrival of big commercial vehicles, which approach the channel from far out at sea and steer a course between 13 large, lighted buoys arranged in two lines, marking a sort of maritime highway.

The buoys are, of course, just as visible to smaller boats like the *Kaught Looking*. Captains of smaller vessels need to use a chart (paper or electronic) and the channel to avoid the jetty, although they sometimes try to cut in someplace in the middle. If they do it too close to the jetty, trouble awaits.

"It's hell on wheels to go close around the corner of the jetty at night," said Richard Wood, who supervises boater safety classes for the Palm Beach Sail and Power Squadron, a maritime educational group. "You can't see anything, there's no moonlight, and the higher the tide, the less the jetty is sticking out of the water. ...

Waters around Government Cut at night, September 26, 2016. (Carl Juste/Miami Herald)

"And if you're out at sea, turning toward the Florida coast, the buoys and navigational lights blend in with every other frickin' light ahead of you – downtown condos, cruise ships, everything you can imagine."

Of course, there's no way – at least not yet – to know whether the *Kaught Looking* was trying to cut a corner into Government

Cut. Perhaps the boat was running alongside South Beach, planning to enter Biscayne Bay from a point south of Fisher Island or Virginia Key, and hit the unseen jetty head on.

Either way, said Wood, the accident shouldn't have happened.

"It was 100 percent preventable, if they knew what they were doing," he insisted. "Though you can't see the jetty at night with your naked eye, you should be watching your chart plotter, the thing we use in boats that's like a GPS in a car. It has a map with a little dot shaped like a boat that's you – it tells you exactly where you are, and where the jetty is.

"And I don't know if the boat was equipped with radar, but that's also very clear. You see an actual radar image of where you are and what you're going into. If it's something solid, that's pretty obvious. Of course, that's assuming it's set properly and you're looking at it. ... If things start to look tricky, you say to yourself, am I too close? Should I turn away? I need to slow down and figure this out."

A terrible noise

Whatever the *Kaught Looking* hit, it hit loud. The collision produced an unearthly screech so violent that a Miami Beach cop on shore reported it to a Miami-Dade County Fire Rescue patrol boat at about 3:20 a.m. A passing Coast Guard patrol boat spotted the wreckage at about the same time, crumpled on Government Cut's north jetty. Divers were in the water within minutes, and by 4 a.m. had recovered all three bodies.

Two hours later, phones began ringing around Miami, and tears started to flow. "I cried and cried," confessed Ozuna, the player who tried to convince Fernández not to go out on the boat. Said Bernal, who fell asleep thinking his worries had been unwarranted: "I just froze. Got goosebumps. A sickening feeling."

The Florida Fish and Wildlife Conservation Commission, which oversees Florida boating regulations, is investigating what caused the accident. "They're going to be trying to create a chronology of what happened," said Wagner, the maritime law attorney.

"They'll be looking at GPS coordinates from the boat's equipment, information on the cellphones the men were carrying. They'll want to know where the boat was coming from and where it was headed. And if that information is time-stamped, they'll be able to tell its speed."

Almost every expert who saw photos of the boat's wreckage had the same immediate reaction: It was traveling fast. Fernández's driving record on land – he was ticketed for driving 82 in a 65 mph zone on the Turnpike in 2013, ran a red light in Tampa later that year, and was cited for swerving into the wrong lane in North Carolina in 2012 – will doubtless be scrutinized. And the results of toxicology tests are expected to be finalized by the end of the coming week.

Many of the same investigative techniques that police use in automobile accidents will be applied to the wreckage of the *Kaught Looking*. "Obviously there are no skid marks to measure," Wagner said. "But depending on the type of incident, the damage to the bottom of the hull, the damage to the propellers and engines, can tell you a lot. If they were torn off, you can tell how, and that may tell you what direction they were headed and what they hit first. ..."

Rocks on the North Jetty show the evidence of the deadly boating accident, September 26, 2016. (Carl Juste/Miami Herald)

"And you'll look at the jetty itself. Paint rubs off in a crash. And with an impact like that, there will be evidence on the rock itself of where the boat first hit."

The position of the boat seems to suggest that *Kaught Looking* was heading south at the time of the collision. But there are other possibilities – notably, that it hit something in the water first, which could have altered its direction. "In maritime situations," Wagner cautioned, "anything is possible."

Even, perhaps, for the sea itself to shed tears. Last week, as literally millions of South Floridians joined Fernández's family in mourning, an odd and heartbreaking package washed up on South Beach, a mile or so from the wreckage of the *Kaught Looking*: a bag of four autographed baseballs, the scrawled name José Fernández still clearly legible.

David Ovalle, David Smiley, Douglas Hanks, Glenn Garvin

Tuesday, October 4, 2016

THE SEA IS JOSÉ'S FINAL RESTING PLACE

The sea that gave José Fernández a new life in Miami, then tragically took it away in a violent boating accident, will – perhaps fittingly – be his final resting place.

According to a report by Radio Martí, a group of Fernández's family and friends scattered the 24-year-old Marlins pitcher's ashes at the site of the crash Sunday, exactly one week since the fatal accident that killed the All-Star and two friends, Eduardo Rivero, 25, and Emilio Macias, 27.

With U.S. and Cuban flags in tow, Fernández's mother, Maritza, deposited his remains at sea, something she said she and Fernández had agreed on. The group paid homage to Fernández in white "José Day" T-shirts and with a lunch in his honor.

Balloons and flowers were left behind at the jetty off South Beach where Fernández's 32-foot SeaVee, *Kaught Looking*, was found early September 25. Since the tragedy, the Miami community turned out in the thousands to honor the late pitcher, who arrived from Cuba at age 15 in an escape by boat that resonated deeply with Cuban exiles.

Chabeli Herrera

Chapter 2

IN MOURNING

Marlins fans pay tribute to their idol at Marlins Park, September 27, 2016. (Pedro Portal/el Nuevo Herald)

Sunday, September 25, 2016

A UNIQUELY MIAMI STORY
From the archives in 2013:

Every game, *abuela* climbs into that sky in Cuba. It is about as close as she ever gets to feeling the freedom her grandson fled to find. Miami Marlins pitcher José Fernández has sent her so many American treasures while trying to bridge the heartbreaking gap now between them. Plasma TVs. Cellphones. A new mattress. He even managed to have air-conditioning installed in grandma's house from afar. But you know what Olga Fernández values most? That radio.

If only for nine innings at a time, it allows her to cross that ocean and feel like she is right next to the All-Star she raised. The island of Fernández's youth rots a little more by the day, and it is stuck in the Dark Ages in many ways, including the televising of baseball. So, because reception isn't great downstairs, up into that sky this 68-year-old lady in Santa Clara climbs with that radio on the nights her All-Star grandson pitches, up there closer to the stars, an old Cuban woman praying that there is no rain while listening to Marlins games alone on her roof.

"I get so emotional," she said in Spanish from her home. "I cry and everything. He takes me with him. It is like I can see the United States through his eyes."

José calls his grandmother "the love of my life ... She's my everything," he said. "There's nothing more important than her." So he enjoys getting the scouting reports from her in their near-daily phone calls.

José's mother, Maritza Fernández, center, and his grandmother, Olga Fernández, before a memorial service at St. Brendan Catholic Church, September 29, 2016. (Roberto Koltun/el Nuevo Herald)

"She tells me, 'The Phillies are good, but you are better,'" José said. "She says, 'Here's the game plan: We're going to go at them hard and away, and low. Stay down in the zone. Breaking balls in the dirt, but not too many because those are bad for the arm.' I told her the other day that they have me throwing 95 to 100 pitches a game, and she screamed, 'What?!' I don't think she knows I'm 6-3, 230 pounds now. She still sees me as 15 years old."

That's not true, actually. She last saw José at that age, before he defected, and didn't even see a new photo of him again until January, when she stared in disbelief at a neighbor's computer.

"My little boy, my love, he is a man now," she said. "He'll always be little to me, but I couldn't even get my arms around him to hug him now, he's so big. He looks so ..."

And the next word she uses tells you a little bit about that gap between our countries.

"Nourished."

A Fearful Place

What was worse, José?

What scared you more?

The two months you spent in a dirty Cuban prison after being caught again trying to defect?

Or the first two months with freedom in America?

"Being here," Fernández said.

How can that be?

"At least in jail I could defend myself," he said. "But here I felt so helpless. Overwhelmed. I've never felt anything worse than my first few months here. Jail felt better than that, and I was in with a guy who killed seven people."

The difficulty of this transition is hard to explain to people who don't understand, though besieged Cuban phenom Yasiel Puig of the Dodgers might try if he had any grasp of English while trying to ward off the build-them-up-tear-them-down-rinse-repeat cycle. Cubans often get here and can't find commonality anywhere but the diamond, where so many of them happen to be fluent. Fernández didn't know the language, the customs, the technology, the people when he arrived here at 15, and he missed his grandmother terribly.

Everything confused him, right down to the smallest things. Like the bathroom faucet at the airport, for example. How were all those people getting water from it? What did they know that he didn't? He stared at the faucet, banging on it, backing away from it, watching others use it successfully. He finally left frustrated, without washing his hands. What did he know about sensors? Censors, he could tell you about. But sensors?

"In Cuba, nobody washes their hands," he said. "There's not even soap."

He got reprimanded for throwing a gum wrapper in the street; he was used to just throwing litter wherever he wanted back home. He didn't know how to turn on a computer. He wrote down phone numbers in a book, not knowing he could program them into his new phone. And high school kids laughed at him for all this, laughed so much that he didn't know when they were laughing at him and when they weren't, all of the laughter sounding the same. So he threw a kid against a fence for calling him Cubanito, not needing to hear anything else.

Fernández's father, Ramón Jiménez — a jokester — told him at the restaurant that he could go up at the buffet and take as much as he wanted. Get out of here, José said, I'm not a sucker. I'm not falling for your tricks, Dad, and getting in trouble. He didn't believe that there was any such thing as all you can eat, not when he came from nothing to eat. No, no, he told the waitress. I did not ask for that, and I will not pay for that. He didn't know anything about free refills.

He could only afford to call his grandmother for three or four minutes at a time. He would skip class, where he didn't understand a word, to go and cry in the woods. He spent nine hours one day sitting in his car by the beach, distraught after learning that his grandmother had again been denied a visa (she has been denied four times).

'A lot of crying'

"I did a lot of crying that I didn't show people," he said. "I asked myself a lot, 'What am I doing here?' I didn't feel like I belonged."

Said his grandmother of those phone calls: "Don't remind me of that please. That made me crazy. I didn't know what was happening with him, and I didn't know how to help him. We'd talk for just a few minutes, and he was not well. I don't want to talk about that time please."

Possible connectors with other students that could have crossed the language barrier: Fernández had no idea what video games even were, never mind how to play them.

"You know how I played in the streets in Cuba? Throwing rocks," he said. "I spent my days picking tomatoes and onions and selling them door to door. I would make a lot of money. Four dollars. That's a lot of money over there. I was really, really poor. But compared to others? Not so poor. I'd walk the 30 minutes to and from the stadium on the street in my cleats because I had only one other pair of shoes, and I didn't want to ruin my going-out shoes."

He sat in a high school class and took the FCAT. Or tried. And failed. He didn't know any of the words, going through a dictionary one by one. Imagine taking a test that way.

"I didn't even know where to write my name," he said. "I put my name in the wrong place."

He asked a fellow student in Spanish for an eraser. The teacher reprimanded him for talking during a test. He knew so few English words, and only the bad ones, so he called her a bitch and got kicked out.

"She later fell in love with José," assistant principal Frank Diaz says now. "Everyone does, you know?"

Baseball was the bridge. Fernández told the coaches he was pretty good in Cuba. Yeah, right, they sniffed; all the new kids say that. They put him in the least-impressive group to try out. He was insulted by that. But then he picked up a baseball ... and so much of the confusion evaporated on the spot.

His coach's reaction?

"Wow," Landy Faedo says now.

Everything changed then. "Before that, no one wanted to talk to me," Fernández said. "Then they saw me playing and everyone wanted to talk to me ... and tried to speak Spanish. ... Girls would come up to me. I don't like popular. I like low-key, humble. But popular is a lot better than lost."

Next thing you know, at lunch, 20 and 30 kids were gathered around Fernández's table, having learned how to play dominoes. Fernández helped Tampa Alonso High School win two state championships.

"He was throwing 94 in the championship game as a sophomore," Faedo said. "That was up from 84-86."

The explanation for the increased velocity?

"He had more food here than there," the coach said. "And he put on weight because he wasn't going everywhere by foot."

Fernández's is a uniquely Miami story, from rags to pitches, with an arm strong enough to pull back in even a scarred and betrayed fan base that keeps getting reasons to pull away. Humble and charismatic, with a child's enthusiasm for joy, he is the only Marlins representative at the All-Star Game tonight, talking through a smile in the kind of accent that surrounds his home ballpark in Little Havana, and with a similar immigrant story.

"He sends me a lot of gifts, but I don't live like a queen here," *abuela* said from Cuba. "I'd live like a queen if I lived there with him. Every day, I pray to be there. It is harder than difficult."

He is a first-round pick, and the owner of a $2 million bonus, and somehow already an All-Star even though he is not yet 21.

Only one thing missing from completing this American dream.

Only one.

You can bet she will be listening Tuesday night in the darkness, up on her roof, searching for a connection 90 and a million miles away.

Dan Le Batard

Monday, September 26, 2016

SHOCK

The grounds crew solemnly stenciled "16" in large white numerals on the pitching mound at Marlins Park before turning on sprinklers to water the outfield grass. They could have collected the tears shed at the ballpark on Sunday to do the same job.

José Fernández's number stenciled in large white numerals on the pitcher's mound at Marlins Park to honor the ace, September 25, 2016. (Courtesy of Marlins Park)

The Marlins were left grieving the loss of Cuban-born pitching sensation José Fernández, who was killed with two others in a boating accident early Sunday morning.

"I'm still waiting to wake up from this nightmare," Marlins slugger Giancarlo Stanton posted on Instagram. "I lost my brother today and can't quite comprehend it. The shock is overwhelming."

Second baseman Dee Gordon was weeping when he arrived at the ballpark for a game that was never played. Manager Don Mattingly and Marlins President of Baseball Operations Michael Hill sobbed when they spoke at a news conference.

All 37 players on the Marlins roster – all but Fernández – stood grim-faced as Marlins President David Samson delivered the devastating news to media.

Marlins President David Samson speaks to the press as distraught President of Baseball Operations Michael Hill, left, and Manager Don Mattingly, right, mourn, September 25, 2016. (Carl Juste/Miami Herald)

"I think that when you talk about a tragedy like this, there are no words that come to mind," Samson said. "There's no playbook."

Fernández was not only the best pitcher on the Marlins. He was one of the premier hurlers in the majors, a 24-year-old flamethrower and two-time All-Star who was as exuberant as he was exceptional.

"When I think about José ... I see such a little boy in him," said Mattingly, fighting back tears. "That's the joy that José played with and the passion he felt about playing."

Fernández was born and raised in Cuba before defecting to the United States on a boat with his mother. During their journey,

Fernández dove into the waters of the Gulf of Mexico to rescue her after she fell overboard during a storm.

The Marlins drafted Fernández with the 14th overall pick in the 2011 draft, and it didn't take long for him to reach the majors. He made his debut at the start of the 2013 season.

Fernández was an instant success.

He captured the National League Rookie of the Year award, was selected to his first All-Star team and became a fan favorite in Miami, where he dominated in his home ballpark.

Fernández missed much of the 2014 and '15 seasons after undergoing Tommy John surgery to repair the ulnar collateral ligament in his prized right arm but picked up this season where he left off, turning in his finest campaign as a big-leaguer.

Fernández was 16-8 with a 2.58 ERA while averaging 12.5 strikeouts per nine innings – the fifth-highest single-season strikeout rate by a pitcher in Major League Baseball history.

"One of the best people I've ever met," Braves first baseman Freddie Freeman said. "Unbelievable competitor. A lot of pitchers, when you get a hit off them, they get mad at you. But he's smiling at you, having a good time. You get drawn to him."

Fernández was originally scheduled to start Sunday against the Braves at Marlins Park, where he owned a preposterous 29-2 career record and 1.49 ERA. But that start – what likely would have been his final outing of the season – was pushed back to Monday. Had the Marlins stuck with their original plans that called for Fernández to start Sunday's day game, it's doubtful he would have gone out that morning on the boat that killed him.

When he spoke to reporters Saturday, Fernández said what he cherished most from the season weren't his statistics, but the fact he had remained healthy, with no arm issues. He tapped his wood locker with his hand when he made the command – for good luck.

On Sunday, hours after the accident, the Marlins were left to deal with the sudden loss.

Samson said the Marlins were first notified about Fernández's accident at about 6:45 a.m.

"Sadly, the brightest lights are often the ones that extinguish the fastest," Marlins owner Jeffrey Loria said in a statement. "José left us far too soon, but his memory will endure in all of us."

While Sunday's game was canceled, Samson said the Marlins would play their remaining six games, albeit with heavy hearts.

"That is how these guys can honor José, and all of us can," Samson said. "I think somebody said that if José were here, he would be saying we're going to get out there [Monday] and play, and honor the game, and honor the people who wish they could play the game but can't."

Marlins third baseman Martin Prado said it will be a difficult time for players.

"We're not robots," Prado said. "We're humans, and we feel. I understand the fact that we've got to play games, and we've got to be professional about it. But in our hearts, there is a lot of pain."

Said Samson: "José, the magnanimity of his personality, transcended culture, religion and race. It just did. His story is a story well-told, and it will be told forever."

Clark Spencer

Tuesday, September 27, 2016

TEARS FLOWING

Dee Gordon did something he rarely does. He homered.

Then he did something he has never done. He cried about it.

On a solemn night when tears were flowing for José Fernández, Gordon – the diminutive second baseman for the Marlins – provided some healing with one shocking swing of the bat.

It brought the crowd of 26,993 – one of the largest of the season – to life at Marlins Park.

And it inspired a team that for the previous 36 hours tried to cope with the numbing loss of their pitching ace and biggest cheerleader. Fernández, who died in a boating accident early Sunday, would have enjoyed every moment of it.

The Marlins wept openly during a pregame ceremony that felt more like a memorial service than a sporting event. Every player and coach wore Fernández's name and No. 16 on the back of their jerseys.

When they took the field, all eight starters touched the chalk line, a Fernández ritual after a win. They stood for the national anthem on the grass perimeter around the same mound where

Fernández had gone 29-2, crying still. Martin Prado cried. Marcel Ozuna sobbed, shaking his head and shielding his face with his cap.

Dee Gordon is consoled by Derek Dietrich, left, after hitting a first-inning home run, September 26, 2016. (Matias J. Ocner/Miami Herald)

Even Giancarlo Stanton, the Marlins' herculean slugger, spent the entire top of the first in right field with tears running down his face.

The crying was everywhere.

Scott Boras, Fernández's agent, was practically bawling when he showed up at Marlins Park.

Others tried to reflect, explain, make sense of something that was beyond understanding.

Marlins President David Samson sat in the dugout, wondering what might have been had Fernández remained on schedule to pitch Sunday instead of being pushed back to Monday in order to safeguard his arm. Had that been the case, it is doubtful Fernández would have gone out on a boat hours before pitching.

"I've been thinking about that a lot," Samson said. "If he had pitched yesterday [Sunday] maybe fate would be different. I've been thinking about that a lot."

His voice trailed off.

There was owner Jeffrey Loria recalling how, after spotting Fernández walking around New York City with his things in a couple of shopping bags after first being called up to the majors in 2013, demanded he buy luggage.

"I said this is not going to work for baseball. It's not going to work for me," Loria recalled. "Tomorrow, you and I are going to the store. We're going to get you the bags and the roller bags you need so you look like a Major League Baseball player."

And they did, with Loria picking up the tab.

There was Manager Don Mattingly, who had broken down at Sunday's news conference as he spoke of how Fernández reminded him of a "little kid," still trying to come to grips with what had happened when he spoke to reporters beforehand.

Don Mattingly during news conference, September 25, 2016. (Carl Juste/Miami Herald)

"We've got to go on, and that's not going to be fun tonight," Mattingly said. "I think guys are still processing how to handle it."

When he was asked if he thought players would rather cancel the team's remaining six games than have to suffer through an emotionally challenging final week, he paused for a moment to give it some thought.

"I don't know," Mattingly said. "I have no idea how to answer that. It might feel good for these guys to come out and play."

And maybe it did.

Maybe it was Gordon, the smallest Marlin, who gave it a kick-start, did something that none of the English- and Spanish-language grief counselors that the team has brought in for players and staff possibly could.

Gordon was the first man up for the Marlins on Monday.

Perhaps no Marlin has shown more sadness and pain than has Gordon.

He was weeping when he showed up at the ballpark on Sunday for a game that was never played. It was Gordon who wore a white R.I.P. T-shirt, with a photo image of Fernández forming the "I" out to batting practice Monday. It was Gordon who placed Fernández's glove and cap next to the rubber as Marlins hitters took their pregame practice swings.

And it was Gordon who brought the Marlins to life in one magical instant.

Gordon, who had hit one fewer homer this season than the Mets' portly pitcher, 43-year-old Bartolo Colon, knocked one of his pitches into the upper deck, and a cloud was lifted.

Gordon circled the bases, touched home plate, and instantly began sobbing as he made his way through the dugout, congratulated by coaches and teammates.

The Marlins scored five runs in the second and another in the third, sending Colon to the showers.

The Marlins won 7-3.

Afterward, they removed their Fernández jerseys, never to be worn again.

Loria said no Marlin will ever wear No. 16 again.

"There are plenty of numbers they can wear," Loria said. "But not that one. We'll let them use triple digits if they have to."

Clark Spencer

Wednesday, September 28, 2016

'HE WASN'T THERE...CHEERING FOR ME'

Adam Conley threw 45 pitches and doesn't remember any of them.

"I don't even know what I did out there," Conley said.

Giancarlo Stanton made four trips to the plate and doesn't remember seeing the ball.

Right fielder Giancarlo Stanton in the dugout during the Marlins-Mets game, September 27, 2016. (Pedro Portal/el Nuevo Herald)

"We were hitting balls from underwater pretty much, our eyes full of water," Stanton said.

Dee Gordon hit a home run and doesn't remember rounding the bases.

"It took forever. It seemed like it took forever," said Gordon, the fastest man on the Marlins.

On a night that none of them will ever forget – what Gordon said was the most difficult game he's ever played in in his life – the Marlins fought sadness and grief to pull out an emotional 7-3 win over the New York Mets.

All any of them could think about was José Fernández, their teammate who was killed in a boating accident the day before.

"I just kept looking over at the ribbon board, kept seeing his name, just kept saying how is he not here?" Gordon said. "Every time I saw his number and name, I kept hearing his voice."

Since all the Marlins wore jerseys on Monday with Fernández's number and name on the back, they often felt like they were seeing his ghost.

"I'd catch a flash of J.B. or Koehler going by [wearing Fernández uniforms], and I was 'there he is,' " Stanton said, referring to teammates Justin Bour and Tom Koehler. "We were waiting for that reality TV show to say they got us."

It was Stanton who gathered his teammates on the field just before the first pitch was thrown and delivered a speech. He doesn't remember much of what he said.

"Honestly, I went kind of numb in that moment," Stanton said. "I don't know if I was stuttering. I don't even know if I was saying the right stuff. A lot of us were talking about, 'Why are we here right now? What's the main purpose of this? How do we get through this together?' I was trying to ease all that, telling them we're all here for José. We're the last hope and the last heart for him, and we need to come together, as hard as it's going to be."

It was a night of hugging and crying.

The Mets came out of their dugout, walked onto the field, and embraced the Marlins before the first pitch was thrown.

Fernández had been scheduled to pitch Monday. That duty fell, instead, to Conley.

"That was José's mound today [Monday night] before I went to take it," Conley said. "He was the starting pitcher today. I didn't go out there. It was José's day to start. And things just changed so quickly."

Conley, who had not pitched in more than a month and was activated from the disabled list in time for Monday's start, pitched three shutout innings before coming out.

"Nothing I felt today had anything to do with pitching," Conley said.

Reliever Mike Dunn took over in the fourth.

"I'm kind of glad I pitched in the fourth because I got it out of the way," said Dunn, who usually appears in later innings. "I didn't have to sit around and think about it. Emotionally I was OK when I was pitching."

But as soon as he completed his inning, Dunn broke down.

"When I got done, I was a train wreck," he said. "I immediately headed for cover [inside the clubhouse]. I sat down, took off my hat, and it just hit me. I bawled like my 11-month-old son. I don't know how the position players did it. I only had to go out there for one inning. They had to play all nine."

Cameras zooming in on Stanton showed him crying throughout the top of the first inning. In the bottom of the first, Gordon purposely took Bartolo Colon's first pitch as a tribute to Fernández.

Gordon belted Colon's second pitch into the upper deck. It was his first home run of the season, and after he circled the bases, touched home plate and returned to the dugout, he started sobbing, because the one player he would have expected to see – Fernández – wasn't there.

"I was just wondering why he wasn't there standing on the top step, cheering for me," Gordon said.

After closer A.J. Ramos took the flip from Miguel Rojas and stepped on first for the final out, the Marlins came out of the dugout for the traditional handshakes.

Marlins hats left on pitching mound, September 27, 2016. (Pedro Portal/el Nuevo Herald)

But there was nothing traditional about what happened next.

Ramos took the ball and placed it on the mound, just behind the rubber.

Then the Marlins formed a circle around the mound, their arms wrapped around each other's shoulders.

They knelt to one knee and bowed their heads.

Then every one of them took off their caps and tossed them on the mound, left them there, and filed back to the dugout and inside the clubhouse.

Manager Don Mattingly bent down and kissed the dirt mound.

"It was saying bye," Mattingly said. "It was his spot. It was just his spot."

Clark Spencer

Thursday, September 29, 2016

ADIÓS, JOSÉÍTO, BELOVED SON OF CUBA, BASEBALL AND EXILE

Miami said goodbye to its fallen baseball star with a dose of *cubanía* as heavy as our hearts.

José Fernández was – on his last ride through the city that embraced him – "Joséíto," the boy who sold onion, garlic and tomatoes on the ramshackle streets of a Cuban town, and against every imaginable obstacle, rose to become a baseball star in the United States.

Cuban-American newsmen choked up on live television Wednesday when they called him that during the farewell – *nuestro Joséíto*. The waitresses who had served him at La Carreta wept as they lined up for a *cafecito* salute along Bird Road when his hearse drove by – and stopped. In a city where emotions easily run high, this was nothing we had ever seen before.

From his teammates to his fans, Miamians from all walks of life mourned his loss as if Fernández were family.

"He was like everyone's son," said Miami Dade College President Eduardo Padrón. "His life was cut short but his light will never dim. ... And for me, his journey to freedom was emblematic of the collective pain of all of us who became men and women overnight in our teens."

Fernández fled Cuba on a boat at 15, his fourth try to leave the country and pursue his dreams in freedom.

Sure, his pitcher's arm was prodigious and, at 24, he seemed destined for Hall of Fame greatness, his fans proudly boast. But it was his human qualities that made Fernández stand out from the rest: A love of family that kept him grounded in his roots and humble despite the millionaire paycheck. A love not only of Cuba but also of the adopted country he fully embraced, becoming a citizen last year.

The night he died he was wearing a T-shirt with the American flag.

Yet his loss is most poignant for the Cuban community. His death is another sad chapter in the long history of the Cuban exile, marked by loss and separation, one exodus after another, and by the rewards of bittersweet successes, too.

Marlins President David Samson and teammates pay respects prior to hearse departing Marlins Park, September 28, 2016. (Carl Juste/Miami Herald)

If, in our six-decade history, Jorge Mas Canosa was the political leader regaled with a statesman's funeral in 1997, and salsa queen Celia Cruz represented our culture and brought thousands of mourners to her vigil at Miami's Freedom Tower in 2003, Fernández marked yet another generation and another entry, sports.

Olga Fernández wearing her grandson's jersey number 16, September 28, 2016. (Robert Koltun/el Nuevo Herald)

At Marlins Park, players in white T-shirts gathered around the black hearse carrying Fernández, arms stretched as if embracing the beloved teammate who died in a tragic boating accident.

They hugged Fernández's mother, clad in black and inconsolable. Then, they saw emerge from the black limousine the petite figure of Fernández's beloved *abuela* Olga, who wore his jersey, No. 16, over black slacks. They sobbed. *Abuela* introduced her grandson to the game as a child, and after they were separated, heard him play in Miami on a radio from her rooftop in Santa Clara. They were reunited three years ago. The Cuban government wouldn't let her leave, but relented after Marlins owner Jeffrey Loria interceded on her behalf at a time when, behind the scenes, there were efforts by both countries to move toward a thawing of Cold War relations.

After a last ride around Marlins Park, the funeral procession headed to the bayside shrine of Our Lady of Charity, Cuba's patron saint, where Fernández's body arrived to canticles to the virgin for a holy water blessing of the casket, condolences, and prayer.

The spiritual home of exiles, *La Ermita* is a refuge for those who seek solace and a connection to the homeland.

But the stop at La Carreta was a touching tribute to Fernández's jovial character. It was the place where he loved to hang out with his people and devour home cooking. A *cafecito* salute to a fallen hero in Westchester, a Miami enclave where working-class exiles moved when they had done just a little better – and, in the process of living, turned their nostalgia for the lost homeland into cultural inheritance.

Oh, what a Miami story he was a part of.

Dan Le Batard

Saturday, October 1, 2016

FERNÁNDEZ'S BAT

Wei-Yin Chen is looking for his first major-league hit, and he hopes to find it in the bag of bats belonging to the Marlins' pitchers. Before taking the mound here on Saturday, Chen plans on rummaging through the bag in search of one bat in particular: José Fernández's.

"Of all the people, he's the one who was most eager wanting to see me get my first hit," Chen said through his interpreter.

Chen presently holds the dubious distinction of being the worst hitter in major-league history. He's never had a hit in 48 career big-league at-bats.

Randy Tate, a pitcher from the 1970s, is next on the list: 0 for 41.

Why, Chen has never even drawn a walk or been hit by a pitch, giving him a career on-base percentage of .000.

For Chen to record his first hit with Fernández's bat would only be fitting.

The two were about as close as any two pitchers on the Marlins, forming their bond in spring training when Chen first joined the Marlins, a Taiwanese left-hander and a Cuban right-hander.

Marlins pitchers Wei-Yin Chen, left, and José Fernández in the Marlins' dugout, June 5, 2016. (Pedro Portal/el Nuevo Herald)

"José was a good friend to all of us," Marlins pitcher David Phelps said. "But him and Chen, they spent more time together than with anyone else in the dugout. You'd see them in the dugout, arms around each other. Those two, they had a little bromance."

Said Chen: "José's actually the first Marlin I met when I came here, so we hit it off very quickly. It was him who introduced me to everybody else."

They went out to eat together. They talked pitching. And, once in a while, they talked about hitting. Fernández was a good hitter for a pitcher, with a couple of home runs and a career .213 batting average. His average this season: .250.

Chen, on the other hand, has been feeble at the plate.

Earlier this season in Milwaukee it looked like his long dry spell had ended when he beat out what was first ruled an infield hit. But the play was later changed to an error, and Chen was left hitless.

"Of all the people, he's the one who is the most eager wanting to see me getting the first hit," Chen said.

"When I couldn't get a hit, when I got off the field, we would talk about the at-bat and sometimes he would encourage me. Sometimes he would mock me and say you [stink]. But he always encouraged me to get my first hit."

Chen said Fernández always beat him, no matter what they were playing.

"All I can say is, he's an amazing athlete," Chen said. "Whatever we played, whether it was basketball with the small basketball we have in the clubhouse, or Ping-Pong; I never beat him. He could do everything."

Even though Fernández was seven years the 31-year-old Chen's junior, he was often the one offering pitching advice, trying to help his friend and teammate.

"This year, I'm having a rough year," Chen said. "If it weren't for him, I might have a worse year than I already have right now. Even though he's younger than me, there was a lot I learned from him."

Chen was looking forward to spending time with Fernández in the offseason.

"We were going to get together for training," Chen said. "And we were going to go out on his boat, and he was going to teach me fishing. We were going to have barbecues. And now it's sad it's not going to happen."

Chen has lost his friend and biggest supporter. He wants to get his first hit more for Fernández than for himself. And he would prefer to do it with one of Fernández's bats.

"That way, I can get my first hit with his bat, because he's just like my brother," Chen said. "That's my way to honor him. I think it would be tremendous for both of us."

Clark Spencer

Chapter 3

INSPIRING STORY

Tampa Alonso High's José Fernández unleashes a pitch late in the seventh inning during the Class 6A regional baseball final at Tampa Plant High School. Alonso won 8-1, May 6, 2011. (Daniel Wallace/Tampa Bay Times)

DRAFTED BY THE MARLINS

Tuesday, June 7, 2011

FIRST ROUND DRAFT PICK

For years, José Fernández and his family dreamed about leaving Cuba behind.

A little more than three years after finally escaping on a tiny boat, another dream came true for Fernández on Monday night.

The 18-year-old pitcher from Tampa Alonso High School was drafted by the Marlins with the 14th overall pick in the first round of Major League Baseball's Amateur Draft.

Fernández, a 6-3, 215-pound right-hander who grew up in Santa Clara, Cuba, has a two-seam fastball, a four-seam fastball that ranges between 92 and 97 mph, a sharp breaking ball and a changeup that is a work in progress.

But none of it may be as good as his story. According to the Tampa Tribune, Fernández tried to flee Cuba four times with his mother and sister, and he spent a year in a jail for those attempts.

"He's faced a lot worse things than anything he'll face going through our system," said Jim Fleming, vice president of player development and scouting for the Marlins. You've got to feel the way he dealt with that, he's going to deal with the day-to-day struggles of baseball very well."

During one attempt to flee, his family was 10 miles off the coast of Miami before being intercepted by the Coast Guard and sent back to Cuba. Another time, his mother, Maritza, fell into the Atlantic Ocean after a wave slammed into their boat. Not knowing who was in the water, Fernández dove in to save a person he knew needed help.

"When you come in that boat, it's hard," Fernández told the Tampa Tribune. "You have to be a man. ... I saw somebody fall from the boat. I didn't even know it was my mom."

According to documents from the U.S. Department of Homeland Security, José, Maritza and his sister, Yadenis, left Cuba for the final time on the night of March 20, 2008. After several days at sea, they arrived in a wooded area near Cancun, Mexico, in a boat holding eight passengers. Days later, they bused to the U.S. border in Hidalgo, Texas, through Vera Cruz and Reynosa, Mexico, reaching their destination April 5.

José Fernández celebrates his first-round Marlins draft with his mother Maritza and grandmother Julia at his home in Tampa, June 3, 2011. (Willie J. Allen Jr./Tampa Bay Times)

What he has already been through is just part of the reason the Marlins believe they drafted a tough, talented, up-and-coming pitcher.

"We liked everything about him," Fleming said. "We saw the film of him. He's a big, strong kid with pitches in place. ... If you know anything about his background, the adversity he's been through, he has a good work ethic. He looks to be good. It was just the kind of a guy that excited from the first day."

Fernández is also a winner. He led Alonso to the Class 6A state championship twice, including last month. As a senior, he was 13-1 with a 1.35 ERA and 134 strikeouts. In three years at Alonso, Fernández was 30-3 with 314 strikeouts.

Fernández is the second pitcher the Marlins have taken with their first pick in the past three years and the fifth consecutive high school player as their first pick.

Manny Navarro

Friday, August 12, 2011

OUTSTANDING WORK ETHIC

José Fernández paces back and forth in the parking lot at Tampa Alonso High, looking for someone to open the gates to the school's baseball field.

It's 8:55 a.m., and the Marlins' 2011 first-round draft pick already has been wondering what to do for a half-hour, as his 9 a.m. workout and bullpen session is scheduled to start in five minutes. An anxious Fernández grabs a bat from his SUV and takes a few cuts to loosen up.

A few minutes later, one of Fernández's advisers, Ken Turkel, pulls up alongside several other cars that dotted the lot. As Turkel steps out of his car, Fernández gives him a quick look. "You're late, bro," Fernández says to Turkel, Team One Management's director of agency relations. "I can't be late when you're standing in a parking lot," Turkel jokes.

"I was here by 8:25," Fernández says. "Fifteen minutes early is on time. On time is late."

This is why Fernández was getting a little antsy about his impending workout: He's fanatical about making sure the timing is right when he trains.

After searching some more, Fernández doesn't seem confident about tracking down a security guard or maintenance man with the magic key. Fernández's other adviser and Team One's director of administration John Agliano jokingly offers an idea: "Why don't you throw here, right on the asphalt? Flat ground, no mound, just like they did in the old days."

For a moment, Fernández smiles. "Nah, man," he says. "That's the way they do it in Cuba. I'm not in Cuba anymore."

Fernández's response puts his past, present and future in perspective.

A native of Cuba, Fernández finally escaped the island on a speedboat with his mother and sister in 2008 after three attempts. The Marlins drafted the 19-year-old right-handed pitcher with the 14th overall pick in June's Major League Baseball Draft, and with time running out before Monday's signing deadline, Fernández might soon have a chance to realize his once-distant dream of playing professional baseball.

Though members of Florida's front office and representatives from Team One declined comment, they are negotiating. If Fernández doesn't sign, he has committed to play collegiately at the University of South Florida.

For now, after another 15 minutes of side chatter and some swings of the bat, Fernández says, "no more waiting." He hops in his green Ford Explorer, drives through a back entrance to Alonso's football field, swings around the back of the stadium and opens a side entrance. Fernández's mother, father, trainer, bullpen catcher and three advisers slowly make their way over to the dugout.

They've now entered José Fernández's office.

Since his high school season ended, and since he was drafted by the Marlins in early June, Tampa Alonso's baseball field is where Fernández has gone to work, seven days a week.

"I just focus on my job," Fernández says. "I know what I've got to do in my life. I've got everything very clear. I've got a good mind. I'm focused."

For three hours each day, Fernández trains with Orlando Chinea, the former Cuban National Team pitching coach who previously worked with big-league pitchers Orlando "El Duque" Hernandez, Livan Hernandez and Rolando Arrojo. Fernández started training with Chinea, whom he calls a second father, three years ago and has added about 15 mph to his fastball velocity.

Almost two months after the draft, only two of the top 16 picks have signed, and during that time Fernández said he has had only one goal: work hard and improve every day.

"I'm not going to lie to you, [Monday] is an important day," Fernández said. "But I'm not really focused on it. I'm just doing what is in my hands. ... That's my job. If I get better, everything will happen on its own. If I work hard and if I throw 100 miles per hour, everything will happen by itself."

After stretching and warming up for about an hour, Fernández heads to the rubber.

Chinea first stands behind Fernández on the infield grass between the back of the mound and second base, dissecting his pupil's every move.

"He has the potential for perfect pitching mechanics," Chinea said. "Everyone said Roger Clemens had a perfect motion, but [José] has better [motion] than Clemens. He was too strong."

Now Chinea wants to get a view from home plate, retreating behind Alvarez and in front an L-screen that serves as protection. Chinea yells instructions every couple of pitches.

"Follow through and finish," he says. Then, "more hand on top." Fernández tweaks the release point on a curveball, snapping off a breaking ball that seemingly buckles the knees of hitters everywhere and registers at 83 mph on Chinea's radar gun. *"Perfecto!"* Chinea exclaims.

"I've never worked with a pitcher like him before. He makes everything click quick," said Chinea, snapping his fingers. "He can make any adjustment."

Throughout the workout, Fernández's fastball hits between 92 and 94 mph, his changeup is between 78 and 80, and his curveball ranges from 69 to 85.

"You want to be perfect. It's hard to be perfect, you will never be," Fernández said. "But when I'm out there, I'm trying to be as close to perfect as possible. I want to be the best. I want to be one of the best pitchers in professional baseball. I'm a human person, but I want to be the best, and that's what I work for. I want to be a machine."

With sweat dripping down his face from underneath a black Florida Marlins hat, and his Alonso "Ravens baseball" T-shirt turning from navy to an even-darker blue saturated with perspiration, Fernández is ready for the last of his 40-pitch workout. Lopez gives a low, outside target, and Fernández hits the spot: 94, on the black. *"Bueno!"* Chinea shouts.

Fernández walks off the bump and into the dugout, changing T-shirts and wiping down his forehead after more than two hours on the field. He estimates that he was throwing 80 percent of maximum effort.

Just another day at work for Fernández, who might have really shown off if someone stepped into the batter's box.

"When I'm out there, I'm a different person. I'm like a lion," Fernández said. "You're going to die, bro. You're not going to get to first base. But if you do, you're not going to get past there. That's my idea, and that's honestly what I think with every pitch. When I'm out there, I'm like an animal."

Matt Forman

Tuesday, August 16, 2011

'I DIDN'T EVEN KNOW WHAT THE DRAFT WAS ...'

When José Fernández fled his native Cuba, he dreamed of freedom. He dreamed of breaking from poverty, dreamed of owning more than "three T-shirts, two pairs of shorts and shoes and one pair of pants." He dreamed of not having to go to jail for saying the wrong thing – or, for that matter, saying anything.

On his fourth escape attempt, taking off on a speedboat with his mother and sister in 2008, Fernández reached Cancun, Mexico, before crossing U.S. border in Hidalgo, Texas. Finally, he could leave home whenever he wanted. He could speak his mind.

"You sit back and think, all those things that you went through, you don't believe it. It's incredible. It's surreal. It's something you don't imagine. It's something crazy," Fernández said. "Being in jail and all that stuff, it's hard. That's not something that a kid at 15 years old should be going through. But that makes you stronger."

Fernández also dreamed of playing professional baseball. But unlike his other dreams, which seemingly were realized after joining his father in Tampa, he didn't exactly know how to accomplish his goal of stepping on a big-league mound.

"I didn't even know what the draft was when I came here," said Fernández, who the Marlins selected with the 14th overall pick in June's draft. "I didn't know anything.

"When I was throwing 94 during my sophomore year, people started noticing and scouts started showing up. People start talking, 'Oh, you could be in the draft. Did you know you could be drafted?' I started looking it up, finding things out, learning a little bit."

Three years later, Fernández has fulfilled another dream. Baseball sources confirmed the Marlins signed their first-round pick roughly two hours before Monday's midnight deadline for $2 million. The sides agreed to a deal about 25 percent more than MLB's slot recommendation, $1,602,000, according to Baseball America. Fernández had committed to the University of South Florida.

José Fernández, center, of Alonso High School, celebrates with his teammates following their 7-5 win over Park Vista at Digital Domain Park, May 20, 2011. (Sam Wolfe/Tampa Bay Times)

Fernández, 19, throws three swing-and-miss pitches: a fastball that rests between 92-96 mph with heavy sink and occasionally touches 99, a knee-buckling curveball that ranges from 69-85 and a low-80s changeup with fade. With a high glove point toward home plate before releasing the ball to keep his front side closed, some scouts have said Fernández looks like Tim Lincecum in mechanics.

Fernández also has a track record of winning. He went 30-3 during his career at Tampa Alonso High School, and led the Ravens to three consecutive appearances in the state championship game, helping the team win the title as a sophomore and senior.

Orlando Chinea, Fernández's trainer and the former Cuban National Team pitching coach who previously worked with big-leaguers Orlando "El Duque" Hernandez, Livan Hernandez and Rolando Arrojo, said he thinks Fernández could reach the major leagues within two years because of his advanced repertoire, pitchability and makeup.

Matt Forman

MINOR LEAGUE SENSATION

Thursday, April 26, 2012

José Fernández, the Marlins' top draft pick (14th overall) last summer, pitched the first six innings of a combined no-hitter for Single A Greensboro (N.C.) on Tuesday.

Clark Spencer

Monday, May 14, 2012

Pitchers José Fernández and Adam Conley, the Marlins' top two draft picks last summer, have yet to lose at Single A Greensboro (N.C.). Fernández is 4-0 with a 1.67 ERA. He has struck out 52 in 43 innings.

Clark Spencer

Monday, May 28, 2012

Single A Greensboro (N.C.) pitcher José Fernández struck out 12 in six innings. Fernández is 5-0 with a 1.67 ERA.

Clark Spencer

Tuesday, June 26, 2012

Five players with ties to South Florida, including two Marlins prospects, have been selected to play in the 14th annual Futures Game, part of the All-Star Game events, July 8 at Kaufman Stadium in Kansas City ... The Marlins' José Fernández (No. 94) is a right-hander who can reach 97 mph and has a slider and changeup that are advanced for his age (19). He is dominating Class A (7-0, 1.59 ERA, 11.4 strikeouts and 2.1 walks per nine innings), and batters are hitting .184 off him.

Walter Villa

Thursday, June 28, 2012

José Fernández, the 19-year-old right-hander who was the Marlins' top draft pick last year, is scheduled to make his debut for Single A Jupiter on Thursday at Roger Dean Stadium. Fernández was recently promoted from Single A Greensboro (N.C.), where he went 7-0 with a 1.59 ERA in 14 starts and struck out 99 in 79 innings.

Clark Spencer

Friday, July 6, 2012

Top pitching prospect José Fernández's second start for Single A Jupiter wasn't much better than his first. Fernández on Wednesday gave up three runs on four hits over five innings. He walked three, hit a batter, and had a wild pitch and a balk. His ERA after two starts: 6.30.

Clark Spencer

Saturday, September 15, 2012

While the Marlins are one loss away from securing their third consecutive sub-.500 season, there was a bit of bright news for the organization on Friday when Baseball America unveiled its 2012 minor-league all-star team. Right-hander José Fernández (first team) and outfielder Christian Yelich (second team) made the list. Fernández went 14-1 with a 1.75 ERA in 25 starts split between the Marlins' two Single A affiliates, Greensboro (N.C.) and Jupiter. As Baseball America noted, Fernández led all minor-league pitchers with a 0.93 WHIP, striking out 158 against 35 walks in 134 total innings.

Clark Spencer

Chapter 4

READY FOR THE BIG LEAGUES

José Fernández before the game against the New York Mets at Marlins Park, April 30, 2013. (David Santiago/el Nuevo Herald)

Wednesday, February 13, 2013

'I'M READY TO PITCH'

Chuck Hernandez knew the instant he saw the Tampa high school senior pitch a couple of years ago that the kid wasn't going to college. José Fernández was just too good.

It was 2011 and Fernández had signed a letter of intent to play at the University of South Florida. But the draft was coming up and Hernandez, a veteran pitching coach for the Rays and Tigers, could tell college wasn't happening, that USF was probably just a backup plan.

"I went and saw him pitch one inning, a high school game during his senior year," Hernandez recalled. "I left after one inning and told [the USF] coach, 'You're not getting that guy. He ain't going to no college.'"

And Fernández didn't. The Marlins took him with the 14th overall pick.

Hernandez, the new pitching coach for the Marlins, was telling the story Tuesday after the hottest pitching prospect in the team's farm system – one of the top prospects in all of baseball – worked off a bullpen mound to sharpen up for the spring.

Fernández, a 20-year-old right-hander, looks like he could be a good one, perhaps the best homegrown pitching talent the Marlins have produced since Josh Beckett more than a decade ago.

MLB.com ranks Fernández as the seventh-best prospect in baseball. ESPN's Keith Law has him listed at 13th overall, seventh among pitchers.

"There's no denying that God blessed him with some good ammunition," Hernandez said of Fernández, who defected from Cuba in a speedboat and barely survived the ordeal. "He's a hard-working kid and he's been through a lot before he ever stepped foot in this country."

Asked whom Fernández reminded him of, Hernandez hesitated. Pressed, he finally conceded that Tigers ace Justin Verlander came to mind.

"Some of the things that make him tick remind me a lot of Verlander, just the way they go about their business, what their focuses are on, what they aspire to do," said Hernandez, who was Verlander's pitching coach in Detroit from 2006 to '08. "But one's there and done it and the other one's working his way towards it."

For Fernández, most believe it's only a matter of time.

"I don't want to go crazy thinking about where I'm going to be, what I'm going to do and where I'm going to go," Fernández said. "I just want to go out there every fifth day, pitch, and help my team win. I don't have any other goals."

Fernández is expected to start the season at Double A Jacksonville, but, assuming he continues to dominate minor-league hitters the way he has the past two years, he could receive his big-league promotion in late summer.

Fernández carries a supreme confidence that reminds some of Beckett back when he was an up-and-comer for the Marlins.

"I want to be the best," he said. "I'm not going to lie. I don't want to be second best. I want to be the best."

José Fernández follows through on a pitch in a bullpen session on the first day of spring training at Roger Dean Stadium in Jupiter, February 12, 2013. (Joe Rimkus, Jr./Miami Herald)

But Fernández isn't resting on his laurels. He worked out three times a day during the offseason near his Tampa home with former Cuban national pitching coach Orlando Chinea.

"I don't see it like, 'All right, I'm better than everybody because I'm [the] No. 7 [prospect] or whatever,' " Fernández said. "I'm just one of the guys competing for a spot here."

As a humble reminder of that, Fernández has been assigned one of the temporary lockers – with a handful of other minor leaguers – out in the middle of the Marlins' crowded clubhouse.

Those players are typically among the first cuts.

Fernández will try to forestall that decision for as long as he can.

"I think my stuff is there," he said. "I'm ready. I'm ready to pitch."

Clark Spencer

JOSÉ'S DAY WILL COME

Thursday, March 14, 2013

José Fernández was all smiles after the Marlins sent him to the minors Wednesday.

The reason?

The Marlins' top pitching prospect – the No. 5 prospect in all of baseball, according to Baseball America – always knew spring training for him was nothing more than a sneak preview of what's to come in the future.

Better days lie ahead.

"They were trying to make it easy for me, and I told them, 'You don't have to. It's not a big deal,' " Fernández said. "I understand how it works. I'm fine."

The Marlins reassigned the 20-year-old right-hander to minor-league camp. But it could be the last time.

When Fernández makes his way to the majors, perhaps by the middle of this season, it could be for good.

"He was impressive," Marlins Manager Mike Redmond said. "He was exactly how everybody described him."

Said Fernández of his brief exit meeting with Redmond and front office executives: "They told me, 'Hopefully, this is the last time.' I'm pretty confident, and I think I can pitch in the big leagues today. That's my personal opinion. Maybe I'm not ready. But that's how I feel.

"I feel I've got to learn, and I've got to do the stuff that will help me be more successful in the big leagues. I think I will."

José Fernández talks with Marlins pitching coordinator Wayne Rosenthal during spring training pitching drills at Roger Dean Stadium in Jupiter, February 28, 2013. (David Santiago/el Nuevo Herald)

Fernández appeared in only one Grapefruit League game, delivering two scoreless innings and allowing one baserunner while striking out two. He also pitched against Venezuela in the country's tuneup for the World Baseball Classic.

"It was fun," he said. "I enjoyed every bit of it, being around big-league guys, pitching against Venezuela. I enjoyed every bit of it, and I'm glad they gave me a chance to be here."

Fernández always knew this day would come. He's just surprised it didn't happen sooner.

"I expected it," he said. "I've been expecting it the last two weeks. I'm 20 years old. I can't be upset. I can't. It's not a secret. I knew I was going to get sent down. I was waiting for it.

"I know I've got to get ready for my [minor-league] season. I want to get my routine going. I knew they made the right call."

Said Redmond: "His day will come."

Clark Spencer

Monday, April 1, 2013

INTO THE MARLINS' STARTING ROTATION

Marlins President of Baseball Operations Larry Beinfest was reading off a long list of roster moves on Sunday when he came to the name he knew would create a ripple.

"Get ready," Beinfest said. "José Fernández. *The* José Fernández."

As in the Marlins' young pitching phenom.

On the day before Opening Day, Beinfest dropped a baseball bombshell by announcing that Fernández — the 20-year-old hotshot, Cuban defector and former first-round draft pick — was not only being put on the team's big-league roster but was also being thrown into the starting rotation.

Fernández will make his major-league debut on Sunday in New York.

"I wanted to laugh. I wanted to cry," Fernández said of his reaction when Marlins owner Jeffrey Loria broke the news to him in a phone call on Friday. "It is crazy."

Pretty much everyone assumed the Marlins wouldn't promote Fernández until later in the season, after some additional seasoning in the minors at Double A Jacksonville. Certainly, there was no indication he would be with the Marlins when they opened their season Monday against the Nationals. After all, Fernández has not pitched above Single A.

But plans changed suddenly when injuries landed not one, but two members of the starting rotation on the disabled list.

Nathan Eovaldi and Henderson Alvarez were each placed on the 15-day DL with right shoulder inflammation.

That created a pair of openings in the rotation. One is being filled by Alex Sanabia, who was called up from Triple A. The other is being taken by Fernández, who is ranked by Baseball America as the No. 5 prospect in baseball. Not since Josh Beckett have the Marlins boasted a pitching prospect with so much promise.

"I think it's been tugging at all of us a little bit," Beinfest said of the decision to bring Fernández to the majors now as opposed to later. "The consensus was this kid is ready to handle it here, he's ready to pitch here."

José Fernández pitches during the second inning of the Marlins-Phillies game at Marlins Park, April13, 2013. (David Santiago/el Nuevo Herald)

Beinfest said Fernández will be placed on a strict limit of 150 to 170 innings this season to protect his arm.

Fernández will also be limited in the number of innings and pitches he can throw each game.

"We understand the asset we have, and the value of him, and his age, and we're going to do whatever we can do to do things in his best interests," Beinfest said. "Our goal is we want him to pitch up here, get the experience now. We think he's ready to do it."

Fernández pitched in only one Grapefruit League game before being reassigned to minor-league camp. But he made the Marlins reconsider after a pair of minor-league outings in which he dominated Double A hitters.

In one, he struck out nine in only four innings. In the other he delivered five no-hit innings.

Fernández proved to be an even greater temptation for the Marlins after Jacob Turner failed to crack the rotation and Eovaldi and Alvarez landed on the DL with what Beinfest termed as "mild inflammation" in their right shoulders. He said MRIs showed no structural damage, and he expects both to be ready to pitch in a month at the latest.

"This has the potential to have some criticism, saying the guy hasn't pitched in Double A, and this and that," Beinfest acknowledged. "I think we understand all those things, and we went through them. But they're all different. Some guys are going to be ready at 24, and some guys are going to be ready at 20. I think we're doing this completely with our eyes open.

"But if you have a special guy that's ready to do it, and he's mature mentally and physically, which we believe he is, we want him to get the experience now.

"We think there's a lot of value in getting experience now, rather than going to Double A."

Manager Mike Redmond said Fernández would be slotted at the back of the rotation, following Ricky Nolasco, Kevin Slowey, Wade LeBlanc and Alex Sanabia. Nolasco is making the Opening Day start for the Marlins at Nationals Park and, with an off day scheduled for Tuesday, again on Saturday before Fernández makes his debut.

José Fernández throws a pitch in the first inning of the game with the New York Mets at Marlins Park, April 29, 2013. (Joe Rimkus, Jr./Miami Herald)

Fernández said he can hardly contain his excitement.

"I'm still in shock," Fernández said. "It's incredible. Knowing that it's not spring training anymore, the season's going to start [Monday] and I'm here with them.

"... It's going to be fun to watch. I've got a lot to learn."

Clark Spencer

Monday, April 8, 2013

ONE OF THE BEST EVER DEBUTS

José Fernández lived up to the hype. The Marlins lived down to their reputation.

The ballyhooed rookie's debut was one of the best ever by a pitcher of his age, but the Marlins squandered the outing by losing

4-3 to the New York Mets on Marlon Byrd's walk-off hit in the ninth.

Fernández "deserved to win that game," said Manager Mike Redmond.

The 20-year-old right-hander made it look easy, retiring the first 10 batters he faced and striking out eight in only five innings.

Asked if anything about the experience came as a surprise to him, Fernández replied: "I really thought it [the feeling] was going to be a lot bigger, like the first inning I was going to be a little nervous. I felt like I was pitching in spring training."

Fernández said the only time he felt nervous was after he left the game and watched innings six through nine from the bench. Fernández turned a 3-1 lead over to the bullpen, only to see it go down the drain.

A.J. Ramos gave up a home run to Daniel Murphy in the sixth that made it 3-2 before closer Steve Cishek lost it in the ninth on Byrd's two-run single with one out.

"This is all on me," Cishek said. "I'm really disappointed."

It wasn't all the bullpen's fault. The Marlins collected 13 hits — 10 off Mets starter Aaron Laffey — but managed only three runs. They stranded 12 and were 2 for 14 with runners in scoring position.

Fernández did his part, at least.

He needed only eight pitches to breeze through the first inning, recording three outs on three fly balls. He struck out the side in the second, and two batters in each the fourth and fifth innings. He caught Ike Davis looking at a called third strike. Same with David Wright.

His fastball was touching 95 mph with consistency and he was throwing all his pitches for strikes, buckling Mets knees with his curve.

Since 1916, only six other pitchers under the age of 21 have struck out at least eight batters while making their debuts, according to baseball-reference.com. Fernández is the first to do it since the Texas Rangers' David Clyde in 1973. Clyde was a Texas high school legend who went directly to the majors without spending a day in the minors.

Fernández didn't spend a whole lot of time there himself. He appeared in only 27 minor-league games since the Marlins took him with the 14th overall pick in the 2011 draft.

Fernández retired the first 10 batters he faced on Sunday before Murphy singled in the fourth.

The Mets finally got to him for a run in the fifth. But that was it.

Because the Marlins are being extra cautious with Fernández, establishing an innings cap on the season of 150 to 170 innings, he was pulled after the fifth.

He totaled 80 pitches, 53 for strikes.

"Phenomenal," said Marlins first baseman Greg Dobbs. "He was really composed, says a lot about him at this stage."

Dobbs said what few Mets hitters reached first (there were only three) all commented on Fernández.

"They all said he's got really good stuff," Dobbs said.

Still, in the end, it all amounted to a loss.

Cishek grazed the front of Ruben Tejada's jersey with an inside pitch that put the first runner aboard for the Mets in the ninth. He then gave up a single to pinch-hitter Kirk Nieuwenhuis that Juan Pierre fielded in left.

But Pierre allowed Nieuwenhuis to go to second with an ill-advised throw to third that was late in arriving and off target. That left Mets at second and third for Byrd, who ripped a line-hugging single to left that scored both and gave New York the victory.

Clark Spencer

José Fernández pitches during the third inning against the Phillies, April 13, 2013. (David Santiago/el Nuevo Herald)

Tuesday, April 23, 2013

PITCHING SNOWBALLS

José Fernández was itching to see snowfall for the first time in his life Monday. But when he takes the mound for the Marlins on Tuesday, he doesn't want to be pitching in the white stuff.

"That's *no bueno*," Fernández said.

The 20-year-old Cuban rookie will be making his fourth big-league start when he faces the Twins in the second game of a split, day-night doubleheader at Target Field – weather permitting.

A storm sweeping across the Upper Plains was expected to blanket the area with as much as eight inches of snow and forced the postponement of the Marlins' game on Monday.

Fernández couldn't wait to see it with his own eyes.

"I want to see it coming down," Fernández said. "My mom was, like, 'Send me pictures! Send me pictures!' "

After the team arrived in Minneapolis on Sunday night, Fernández reached down to touch some of the stuff that was already on the ground, but was warned off by a couple of his teammates, Placido Polanco and Donovan Solano.

"They were, like, 'Wait for [Monday],' " Fernández said. "It was so dirty."

Snow is only one of the surprises Fernández has discovered during his brief time in the majors. The other: "The game humbles you really fast," he said.

After two sparkling outings to begin his career, Fernández was brought to earth in Cincinnati when the Reds got him for four runs in a single inning. The Marlins' boy wonder – the youngest starting pitcher in franchise history – tasted his first defeat.

Afterward, a few of the Marlins' veterans told him to relax, that it wasn't the end of the world.

"They sat me down, and they talked to me," Fernández said. "They said, 'Papa, welcome to the big leagues. It's going to happen many times. It's just how you react to it. It's how you get ready five days later. If this would have happened last year, I would have still been crazy about it."

Marlins Manager Mike Redmond said there's a polish and demeanor to Fernández that defies his age.

"You don't look at him and go, 'Man, that's a 20-year-old kid,' " Redmond said. "For a 20-year-old kid to have the command, and be able to throw a 2-1 breaking ball or 3-2 breaking ball for a strike – or a change-up – whenever he wants for a strike? That's special. That's the stuff that's going to make him a true No. 1 pitcher."

Redmond was a catcher with the Marlins the last time they had a young pitcher so promising, Josh Beckett, make his way to the majors. But Redmond said Beckett and Fernández, other than their potential at such a young age, are so different in style.

"Josh loved the fastball, which was good, too," Redmond said. "He was aggressive and it was 95, here it comes. I'll throw my curveball every once in a while and my changeup. But it's mostly fastball/breaking ball, and that's how he pitched."

Fernández has a four-pitch arsenal that he's willing to use at any time. Because Fernández is so confident in throwing all of his pitches, Redmond said it also can get him into trouble. Redmond said that sometimes it might be better for Fernández to use his fastball more the first time through the lineup before shifting gears by going to his breaking stuff the second and third time through.

"Sometimes, when you throw a lot of breaking balls, you have a tendency to elevate your pitch count," Redmond said. "Those are all things he's going to learn."

At this point, pretty much everything is a learning process for Fernández.

He didn't pack enough warm clothing and planned to make a shopping trip to get him through the next couple of days before the Marlins return home.

If the weather is frigid Tuesday night when he takes the mound, he said he'll deal with it.

"I'm not worried," he said. "I'm not. Sometimes you expect a young guy, like, how's he going to react after he gives up six runs? How's he going to do? And I'm not worried. I'm just going to go out there and enjoy it."

Clark Spencer

Wednesday, April 24, 2013

FRIGID DAY OF FRUSTRATION

It was a bone-chilling 38 degrees when José Fernández took the mound at Target Field on Tuesday. The Minnesota Twins didn't make the rookie feel any warmer.

Oswaldo Arcia tagged his first major-league home run off Fernández – a three-run shot in the fourth inning – as the Twins won the first game of a split, day-night doubleheader, 4-3.

Fernández suffered his second consecutive loss while the last-place Marlins fell to 4-16, the franchise's worst-ever record at the 20-game mark.

Ricky Nolasco was scheduled to start the first game of the split doubleheader, with Fernández going in the second. But the Marlins decided to flip-flop the two pitchers Tuesday morning.

Manager Mike Redmond said the organization wanted the inexperienced Fernández, 20, pitching during the warmer daylight hours and the more seasoned Nolasco pitching at night when it was expected to be even colder.

"When we saw the sun shining [Tuesday morning following snowfall overnight], it just made sense to push Fernández up to start Game 1, a little bit warmer," Redmond said. "Ricky's a little bit more accustomed to throwing in colder temperatures."

Multiple sources said the decision was made by higher-ups in the organization, however, and did not sit well with Redmond, pitching coach Chuck Hernandez and Nolasco, who were all caught off guard by the announcement.

For doubleheaders, it is normal protocol to allow the pitcher with the most seniority to have the choice of games.

Nolasco is the Marlins' all-time leader in games started and wins. Fernández had made only three big-league starts. And Nolasco's name was on the lineup card Tuesday morning when players began showing up at the ballpark.

"Not a smart move," said a member of the Marlins' uniformed contingent. "It's a slap in the face to Ricky."

The team member said the perception is that Fernández received preferential treatment because he is the organization's "new golden boy."'

Fernández was just as oblivious to the change in plans. He said he received a call at 9.30 a.m. notifying him of the change.

Fernández was not sharp Tuesday on what was the fifth-coldest game-time temperature in Marlins history.

Brian Dozier ripped Fernández's second pitch of the game into the gap for a triple and ended up scoring on Justin Morneau's ground-ball out.

Joe Mahoney gave the Marlins a 2-1 lead with his two-run single off Twins starter Kevin Correia in the fourth.

But the Twins then went on the attack in their half of the fourth. Chris Parmelee reached on a first-pitch single, Trevor Plouffe followed with another first-pitch single and Arcia connected crushed a first-pitch changeup over the wall in right.

"It was three pitches, three runs – boom-boom-boom," Fernández said. "I looked back, 4-2 we're down."

Fernández was lifted after the fifth.

"We just had a chance to win, and I just kind of blew it up," Fernández said. "It doesn't feel good. I like to give the team a shot to win. It was pretty tough [Tuesday]."

The Marlins loaded the bases with one out in the eighth after Placido Polanco and Giancarlo Stanton were struck by pitches. But they managed only one run. Greg Dobbs ripped a line shot up the middle that appeared headed to center for a two-run single. Instead, pitcher Jared Burton reached up just in time. The ball struck his glove, caromed to short and Dobbs was thrown out at first.

Clark Spencer

Saturday, May 4, 2013

DEVELOPING THE PRODIGY

José Fernández was ecstatic after being formally introduced Friday to his major-league pitching idol, Phillies lefty Cliff Lee, even though their pitching styles are not at all alike.

"I told him, 'I don't know why you're my favorite pitcher because we don't have the same stuff,' " Fernández said. "And he was looking at me like, 'Yeah, you're right.' He goes about his business, doesn't care about anything else. I just like the way that he pitches."

Among other things, Lee also does something with a regularity that Fernández longs to emulate: finish what he starts. Over the past five seasons, only Philadelphia teammate Roy Halladay has totaled more complete games than Lee.

With the Marlins keeping a short leash on Fernández to further the development of their 20-year-old prodigy, the young pitcher's recent outings have been brief, which has put a strain on the bullpen.

He'll be taking the mound for the Marlins on Saturday at Citizens Bank Park for his sixth big-league start.

Fernández was lifted from his previous start after throwing 81 pitches in only four innings of a game that ended up going 15 innings.

Fernández has thrown no fewer than 79 pitches – but no more than 85 – in any of his five starts so far this season.

"I think we'll bump him up a little bit here as we go," Marlins Manager Mike Redmond said.

"We have a plan. We've just been kind of playing it by ear."

The Marlins intend to limit Fernández to 150 to 180 innings this season, and Fernández understands their logic.

"If they give me 200 pitches a game, I'm going to take that," Fernández said. "If they give me 120, I'm going to take that, too. But I respect everything they're doing, and I'm pretty happy with how things are going. They know what's best for the team. I don't ask."

Clark Spencer

Sunday, May 5, 2013

FIRST MAJOR LEAGUE VICTORY

A year ago, José Fernández and Marcell Ozuna were tearing it up in the low minors, far from the spotlight of the majors. On Saturday, the two youngest Marlins put it to the Philadelphia Phillies in front of 40,091 at Citizens Bank Park.

Fernández, 20, pocketed his first major league victory, delivering seven shutout innings as Marlins pitchers combined on their first one-hitter since 2011 while Ozuna, 22, clobbered his first big-league home run in a 2-0 triumph over the Phillies.

It marked only the third time the Phillies have been one hit in their home park, which opened in 2004. They have never been no-hit there. For the Marlins, it was the 15th one-hitter in franchise history.

All that separated the Marlins from the franchise's fifth-ever no-hitter – albeit a combined effort had it occurred – was a Freddy Galvis single with one out in the first inning.

After that, Fernández took over, retiring 17 consecutive Phillies before issuing a leadoff walk in the seventh. He then closed out his performance by whiffing Chase Utley, Ryan Howard and Delmon Young.

"He is really impressive," said Phillies starter Cole Hamels, who gave up only four hits over eight innings in taking the loss. "He is going to be a really great pitcher for a really long time. He has a power heater, power curveball, a pretty good curveball, and he's not afraid. He's going to put up some pretty big numbers in his career."

Marlins catcher Miguel Olivo said Fernández on Saturday reminded him of Ubaldo Jimenez with the Rockies in 2010, the way he had every pitch working. He also said the Phillies hitters kept telling him how impressed they were with him.

"They keep saying, 'Man, he's nasty,' " Olivo said.

Fernández totaled only 82 pitches yet struck out nine Phillies before departing for a pinch-hitter in the eighth. The Marlins are capping Fernández's pitch count by design, given his age.

"He had done his job," Marlins Manager Mike Redmond said. "It really wasn't a tough decision to take him out of there."

Fernández was coming off a pair of so-so outings in his two previous starts but was champing at the bit to get back on the mound Saturday.

"I look forward to every start like it's going to be the World Series," Fernández said. "It's been a lot of work, fixing a lot of things, learning a lot of things."

Fernández received a little offensive help from his former teammate on the 2012 Jupiter Hammerheads when Ozuna led off the second inning by swinging at Hamels' first pitch and landing it in the seats in left-center.

Ozuna's family, who had flown from the Dominican Republic to see him in person, stood and applauded at their seats.

In the third inning, Chris Valaika also homered for only the second time in his career. That gave the Marlins a 2-0 lead that held up to the end when relievers Mike Dunn and Steve Cishek closed out the victory by blanking the Phillies over the final two innings.

The Phillies probably aren't looking to face Fernández again anytime soon. In their two games against him, he's given up three hits over 13 combined innings while striking out 14 and walking just three.

"It's amazing to get a win," Fernández said. "But, for me, it's more important for the team than for me. I was just trying to throw strikes and get outs."

Clark Spencer

Tuesday, May 28, 2013

LEARNING FROM FAILURE

Homecoming was a disaster for José Fernández.

Playing only a short distance from the Tampa home where he spent his teenage years, in front of a throng of his friends and former teachers from nearby Alonso High, the young rookie for the Marlins turned in the worst performance of his budding major-league career.

"It hurts," Fernández said Monday after giving up seven runs – four earned – in a 10-6 loss to the Tampa Bay Rays. "It's good to come back home. I'm sorry it didn't come out the way it should. I tried my best."

Fernández, 20, was making just the 10th start of his fledgling career.

But the kid didn't have it, walking the first two batters he faced in a disastrous second inning, plunking the third and allowing six runs before he was able to finish the frame.

The inning left Fernández perplexed and scratching his head.

"Weird inning," he said. "I don't know what happened in the second inning. Maybe I was trying to be too fine, and that's what happened."

Marlins Manager Mike Redmond thinks he knows the cause: In trying to impress and dazzle his large contingent of followers, Fernández probably overdid it and paid the price.

"He was overthrowing," Redmond said. "He threw a couple of fastballs – I think he hit 99 a few times. That's great on a radar gun. But that shows me he's trying to do a little bit too much."

Fernández capped off a three-strikeout first inning by whiffing Rays star Evan Longoria on a 99-mph high heater but came unglued in the second. After his lack of control caused him to load the bases, he fell apart even further, giving up an RBI single to Yunel Escobar, another run on a safety squeeze bunt by Ben Zobrist that was played poorly by catcher Rob Brantly and a three-run home run to Kelly Johnson – one of two such three-run blasts for Johnson in Monday's game.

"He just couldn't get it back together after that," Redmond said.

Despite the early 6-0 deficit, the Marlins managed to battle back and pull within a run, 7-6, by scoring three runs in the fourth inning off Rays starter Jake Odorizzi and three more in the fifth. But they couldn't get over the hump and went down to their sixth consecutive loss.

Although their bats showed some rare life Monday, with every member of the lineup contributing at least one hit and the team totaling 11, the Marlins made their share of mistakes, too.

Take Zobrist's safety squeeze with one out in the second. Brantly fielded the bunt cleanly in front of the plate but tried to get greedy and threw to second in an ill-advised bid to get a double play. His throw pulled Adeiny Hechavarria off the bag. A run scored, and everyone was safe.

"That's one of those plays where he got the ball and he just didn't look," Redmond said of Brantly. "He didn't look at the runner at third base. He could have run him back, and it's an easy play.

"But he tried to turn a double play, and I think we got a little exposed there on some of our inexperience."

The Marlins also had a high, infield fly land amid a trio of fielders for a double. That ball might have gotten lost in the white roof at Tropicana Field. And when reliever Dan Jennings didn't bother to hold Johnson at second as he was purposely walking Longoria, Johnson stole third on the fourth pitch of the intentional walk.

But the story was Fernández.

"Will he remember this outing? I'm sure," Redmond said. "Will he build off it? Absolutely. He'll be a better pitcher down the road, even though [Monday] was a tough one to swallow for him."

Said Fernández: "The most important part is I'm learning from it."

Clark Spencer

Sunday, June 2, 2013

ROOKIE REIGNS

After picking up his mother at the airport Saturday and taking her to lunch, José Fernández did what a 20-year-old son is supposed to do: He made her proud.

Fernández not only recorded his first home win with a dominating performance on the mound, but delivered two big hits at the plate as the Marlins rolled to an 8-1 victory over the New York Mets.

"Anytime I get to see my family, that makes me really happy," he said.

The rookie hurler turned in seven shutout innings, retired the final 11 batters he faced – seven on strikeouts – and proved to the Mets he's not someone they'll look forward to seeing in the years to come.

If the Marlins fail to challenge the hapless 1962 New York Mets for incompetency, they can thank the modern Mets for helping them out. They have proved to be the only team the Marlins have managed to beat with any regularity.

On Saturday, the Marlins – winners of 15 games all season – defeated them for the fifth time.

While Fernández was doing his thing on the mound, holding the Mets to three singles while whiffing eight, the Marlins hitters showed some rare spark at the plate by pounding out 13 hits.

It was a collective effort, too.

Every member of the lineup, save for Juan Pierre and Marcell Ozuna, collected at least one hit. Eight different players scored a run, with only Adeiny Hechavarria failing to cross home plate.

And the Marlins were aggressive on the base paths.

Catcher Jeff Mathis scored from first on a Fernández single to left-center in the second and drove in a run with a triple in the fourth. The triple for Mathis was just his second in 1,437 career at-bats. Only two other active players with at least 1,400 at-bats, Justin Smoak and Chris Snyder, had either one or zero triples going into Saturday.

Marlins manager Mike Redmond congratulates José Fernández after defeating the St. Louis Cardinals 5-4, June 14, 2013. (Pedro Portal/el Nuevo Herald)

"It was a good day offensively," Manager Mike Redmond said. "Everybody stepped up, and I'm happy to see that. It was good that we could distribute it."

But it was Fernández who set the tone with his work on the mound.

Fernández was emerging from the most disappointing outing of his career when, while pitching in front of dozens of friends and family members on Monday in St. Petersburg, he gave up seven runs and was knocked out in the fourth inning by the Tampa Bay Rays.

"I was a little upset like I should be after that game," Fernández said.

Fernández was perhaps too amped up for that game, and it cost him.

"He was probably overly excited, probably trying to do a little too much," Mathis said.

With Fernández, Mathis said, "All the talent's there, and we all see that."

The key for the pitcher, Mathis said, "is just putting the governor on himself, just staying within himself."

Fernández was never not in control Saturday. Taking on the Mets for the third time already, Fernández gave up a leadoff single to Omar Quintanilla to start the game before going into shutdown mode.

When he reached the fourth inning, he gained command of his curveball and the Mets became helpless to do anything about it.

"Took him a little while to settle in and get his secondary pitches to come around and be able to throw those for strikes," Redmond said. "I know his fastball was good early. But he really started throwing his breaking ball, and once he got that going, he was in complete control of the game."

Redmond was also pleased that Fernández was able to put the Rays outing behind him.

"He's been able to bounce back after a tough start and be great, and he was again [Saturday]," Redmond said.

Said Fernández: "I controlled myself, not overdo myself. I'm pretty happy about how I came back."

The win put the Marlins in a rare position. With a win on Sunday, they would claim their first series sweep and first three-game-winning streak.

Clark Spencer

Tuesday, July 2, 2013

ANOTHER GEM BY FERNÁNDEZ

If 20-year-old Marlins pitcher José Fernández repeats performances like Monday's 4-0 snuffing of San Diego, a pitcher raised in the era of ubiquitous video might throw pitching preparation back to the days of daytime World Series games.

Fernández took copious notes on the Padres throughout the first three games of the series. Then, he told catcher Jeff Mathis during their pregame meeting, "This time, I didn't look at the videos. I didn't do anything. I trust you. I know you're going to do your stuff."

Mathis did his stuff – "I checked him one time. It was the last guy I faced because I wanted to throw one changeup in the game" – and Fernández did his. He gave up only two hits, struck out 10 and walked only one in eight innings, then bounced around the dugout while A.J. Ramos and Steve Cishek took care of the ninth.

Fernández (5-4), who said he felt good after five pregame pitches, gave up a double in the first but struck out the side in the second.

"It was incredible, tempo-wise," Fernández said of the chemistry he had with Mathis. "You're just throwing. He's calling, you're throwing."

After the Marlins broke through on San Diego starter Jason Marquis with an RBI single by Marcell Ozuna in the sixth, Mathis brought in three runs with a two-out double. That gave him seven RBI in his past two bases-loaded situations. He homered Sunday to give the Marlins a walk-off win.

Marquis (9-4) did his part to keep the pace quick in the 2-hour, 27-minute game. The Marlins didn't get a hit until the fifth inning.

David J. Neal

Chapter 5

ALL-STAR

José Fernández holds his National League All-Star jersey before the game against the Washington Nationals at Marlins Park, July 12, 2013. (David Santiago/el Nuevo Herald)

NAMED TO ALL-STAR SQUAD

José Fernández was just a teenager when he etched the number "99" on a mirror inside his home in Tampa. It wasn't a favorite number. It wasn't a lucky number. It was the speed he wanted for his fastball.

"When he was starting high school, he wrote that number on the mirror, so as to see it when he got up every morning, and to remind him that every time he combed his hair or looked at himself, that it was the number of miles per hour he wanted to reach on his pitches," said Ramón Jiménez, José's father.

"José has always been like that. When he fights for something, he never lets down his guard."

It is that kind of determination and drive that put Fernández — a 20-year-old who five years ago fled communist Cuba in a speedboat and is now a rookie pitching sensation with the Miami Marlins — in this year's coveted All-Star Game. Named to the National League squad late Saturday, he's the youngest Marlin ever to be named to the All-Star team.

"It's just incredible," Fernández said on Saturday from St. Louis, where the Marlins are playing the Cardinals. "When they told me, I just started sweating and my hands started getting cold. They still are right now. I was just sitting around and thinking this is just incredible. I'm going to do the best I can."

It was just a little more than three months ago that he made his pitching debut against the New York Mets. In a few short months, he has become one of the main attractions in an otherwise dismal Marlins season.

The Marlins, under public scrutiny after finishing last in 2012 and releasing valuable and experienced players, are thrilled at having another potential Dontrelle Willis on the mound.

"I look at José and I can't avoid comparing him to the D-Train. I see it in his look, his confidence, in the joy with which he looks at life," said Marlins manager Mike Redmond, who caught for Willis in that magical season in 2003 when the team won the World Series and Willis was named National League Rookie of the Year. "Every time he pitches, something almost magical happens, something good is expected and his teammates feel that way. José gives us a big chance of winning."

On a team with barely 32 wins, the kid from Santa Clara, Cuba, has a 5-4 record and a 2.72 ERA — the best of any rookie and 10th-best in the National League — yet nothing describes his dominance better than these statistics: 94 strikeouts in 92.2 innings.

Beyond the numbers, Fernández goes to the mound with an aggressive attitude. At 6 feet 2 inches, and weighing 240 pounds, he wants to intimidate the batter, from the moment he raises his glove to cover his face to when he delivers the pitch — as if he were going back to the times of a Roger Clemens or a Bob Gibson.

"At home we used to tell him that he was a big child, but the truth is that José has always behaved as an older person and his maturity startled us," said Jiménez, who took on the role of a father when José was only 3 months old and has remained at his side ever since. "Since the first time I had him in my arms, I felt something special for the kid. Now I see him pitching, wearing the Marlins uniform and I'm so proud, because the road to get here has not been easy for him or me."

The road to America began in Cuba, where Fernández started playing baseball at age 5. By age 14, according to the Tampa Bay Times, he had pitched in three national championship games. He was enrolled in the Villa Clara Province's School for Sports Initiation (EIDE) and appeared destined to join the Cuban National Team, reported the Times.

Fernández — who does not have a close relationship with his biological father — had made several attempts to leave Cuba. Following one attempt, he spent a year in prison for "illegally attempting to leave the country," he said.

"I am always asked these days if pitching for the Major Leagues makes me nervous or gets me restless, but none of that happens," said Fernández, who at 20 years and 250 days old is this season's second youngest player, second only to Bryce Harper (20 years, 173 days). "I've gone through a lot of experiences that have not always been positive, though they have made me stronger. Pitching at this level does not scare me. On the contrary, it's something I respect and value and also enjoy."

Fernández, who turns 21 on July 31, said he will never forget the day he boarded a boat for his fourth attempt in 2008 to flee

Cuba. He and his family were determined to leave at all cost to reunite with Jiménez, who had left in 2005 after making 14 attempts.

During that journey something happened that left a mark on Fernández for the rest of his life.

After escaping flying bullets from Cuban coast guard boats, and later in the solitude of the ocean on their way to Mexico, somebody said that a person had fallen in the water. Fernández did not hesitate and jumped in. When he finally had the fallen person in his arms he was shocked to realize that he had just saved his own mother, Maritza.

"I have always been a good swimmer, since I was a kid, which is why I am always alert," Fernández said. "I dove to help a person not thinking who that person was. Imagine when I realized it was my own mother. If that does not leave a mark on you for the rest of your life, I don't know what will."

Fernández, Maritza and his sister, Yadenis, spent several days at sea before arriving ashore near Cancún, Mexico. They rode a bus to the U.S.-Mexico border in Hidalgo, Texas, traveling through Vera Cruz and Reynosa, Mexico. They finally set foot in the United States on April 5, 2008, later settling in Tampa with Jiménez.

In Tampa, stories began to circulate about a pitching phenom from Cuba who dominated batters his same age. At age 18, he finished high school with a 30-3 record, recording 314 strikeouts and giving up only 59 walks. In his last three years, he led Tampa Alonso's Ravens to two Florida state titles in Class 6A. He closed his high school career with a 13-1 season and two no-hit games.

A big part of the kid's success is attributed to Orlando Chinea, an almost legendary pitching coach from Cuba who manages a baseball academy in Tampa that has trained dozens of pitchers.

"I'm not surprised by José's success and I don't exaggerate when I say that he could become the best Cuban-born pitcher ever," said Chinea, who had coached the best pitchers on the island and later worked for years in baseball in Japan.

"It's not only the obvious physical maturity but his mental strength. He is ready to face any situation and move forward. We are only looking here at the surface of his talent."

Drafted by the Marlins in the first round of the 2011 amateur draft, Fernández did not disappoint, winning Rookie of the Year in his first season with farm teams.

Even so, many believed that the Marlins were making a mistake by promoting a kid who had never pitched beyond Class A to the majors, and had less than 200 innings in the minor leagues.

Now all those doubts have disappeared with his convincing performances. And his pitching prowess has earned him a trip to New York's Citi Field, home to this year's All-Star game July 16.

He certainly won't be a stranger at Citi Field. It's the same stadium where he made his Major League debut on April 7.

Jorge Ebro

Sunday, July 7, 2013

FUTURE 'FACE OF THE FRANCHISE'

José Fernández hasn't had to calm down too often during a start this season.

He had to for a moment Saturday afternoon after stepping into his manager's office.

Fernández, the Marlins' 20-year-old talented rookie pitcher, had just found out he was an All-Star.

Fernández found out from Marlins owner Jeffrey Loria, who called in to Marlins manager Mike Redmond's office after Saturday's game as Redmond and Marlins vice president/general manager Mike Hill were listening.

Redmond said earlier this week that Fernández could one day be the "face of the franchise."

Fernández will get a taste of what that feels like July 16 in New York as the Marlins' lone representative selected to this year's All-Star Classic.

Only 25 days away from his 21st birthday, Fernández became the youngest Marlin to be named to the All-Star Game. Miguel Cabrera was 21 years and three months old when he was picked in 2004, and Dontrelle Willis was also 21 when he earned his first All-Star nod in 2003.

Fernández, who is set to start the series finale Sunday against the Cardinals, is 5-4 with a 2.72 ERA in 16 starts and has 94 strikeouts to only 33 walks. His ERA is the best in the majors among rookie starting pitchers, and his strikeouts rank second among rookie pitchers overall, behind the Cardinals' Shelby Miller (107).

"I got lucky to be picked and be with those incredible players and learn from them the most I can," Fernández said. "I think it's going to be a great experience, and I'm going to enjoy it."

José Fernández during the beginning of a game against the Mets, July 31, 2013. (David Santiago/el Nuevo Herald)

In his last start July 1 against the Padres, Fernández became only the third pitcher since 1921 to record at least 10 strikeouts while allowing two hits or fewer and walking one batter or fewer in a game, joining Dwight Gooden (1984) and Kerry Wood (1998).

Fernández had been rumored to be the most likely candidate for the Marlins' mandatory spot on the National League roster during the past couple of weeks.

"I didn't want to think about [getting picked]," Fernández said. "It was all really hard not to think about it. I was just trying to go out there and pitch it start by start and get my job done and help the team win. That's my main goal every time."

But Fernández took a moment to reflect on the five-year journey he has taken from his native Cuba to become an All-Star. Fernández's success, coupled with his story of courage by surviving four attempts to flee Cuba including the near-drowning of his mother, has resonated around baseball this season.

"It's just something that I've wanted to do in my career," Fernández said. "This is playing with the best players in the world. When I think about it, it's something that I'm going to remember for the rest of my life."

Andre C. Fernandez

Wednesday, July 17, 2013

ALL-STAR STAR

As far as All-Star debuts go, there aren't many pitchers in the history of the game who put on the type of show Marlins rookie José Fernández did Tuesday night at Citi Field in the American League's 3-0 victory.

In fact, only two others did — Dwight Gooden and Bob Feller. That's the company the 20-year-old Cuban defector joined in the sixth inning when he sandwiched strikeouts of former MVP Dustin Pedroia and current major-league home run leader Chris Davis around getting Triple Crown winner Miguel Cabrera to pop out.

Gooden and Feller, two of the top 50 strikeout kings in the history of the game, are the only other players to manage to do that before their 21st birthday.

"Dangerous group of hitters there," Fernández posted on his Twitter account moments after exiting the game. "I felt like I was going to throw 110."

Fernández, who wore bright orange shoes with his Twitter handle on them, didn't hit 110 on the radar gun. But he came close.

On the big stage just a few months after he was surprised to make the jump from Single A to the big league team on Opening Day, he hit 98 mph three times on the radar gun against Cabrera, a former Marlin. His strikeouts came on a 96-mph two-seamer at the knees against Pedroia and then a nasty curveball against Davis, who has slugged 37 homers this season.

In all, only five pitchers have made an All-Star appearance before their 21st birthday. Fernando Valenzuela and Jerry Walker are the others.

"It's an honor to be mentioned with those guys," Fernández said.

Earlier in the day, Fernández reached into his locker Tuesday afternoon at Citi Field and pulled out a white Marlins jersey to show a friend.

This wasn't any ordinary jersey, though. It had the autographs of every All-Star in the National League clubhouse on the back of it, a special keepsake the 20-year-old rookie said he planned on putting in a frame and on a wall up in his house.

"I got a bat autographed, too," Fernández said with a smile on his face. "It's been amazing just to be here talking to all these guys."

The second-youngest player and the only rookie at this year's All-Star Game, Fernández spent his first 48 hours in New York busy conducting interviews in both English and Spanish, and signing tons and tons of autographs himself.

"It's been crazy — nothing but signing and talking, signing and talking — a lot of stuff to sign," Fernández said. "But I'm not complaining. I'm thrilled to be here."

Fernández, the youngest Cuban-born player in baseball history to earn an All-Star nod, said he had a great time Monday catching up with fellow Cuban defectors Aroldis Chapman and Yoenis Cespedes. They stayed on the field talking even after the National League had already completed its pregame workout.

Fernández said he didn't know either until this trip to New York, but he had heard about their big-time talent while he was growing up in Cuba. Their stories of defection, though, weren't nearly as harrowing as his.

Chapman, 25, and now a two-time All-Star for the Reds, walked out on the Cuban National Team during a tournament in the Netherlands in 2009. Cespedes, who received a special invite to the All-Star Game for the Home Run Derby and edged out Bryce Harper to win it Monday night, fled Cuba with his family for the Dominican Republic in 2011. He's now 27.

Fernández was 15 when he jumped into the waters of the Gulf of Mexico to save his mother during his fourth and final attempt to escape to the United States. Before that, he spent months in prison next to murderers, locked up because he sought a better life and tried to leave a communist country.

"We talked like we've known each other for 10 years," said Fernández, who cheered on Cespedes during the derby.

"A lot of guys were impressed by the way Cespedes hit the ball last night. He was hitting them like nothing, like he was in a Little League park. I really enjoyed it. [Cubans] just love the game, respect it and play hard."

Fernández, who brought his mother with him on his All-Star trip, said the first thing he plans to do when he gets back to Miami is call his grandmother in Cuba to share his experience. She was listening to the game on radio on the roof of her home.

After Tuesday night, though, the focus will return to the Marlins. Just the third Marlins rookie to make the NL All-Star team (joining Dontrelle Willis and second baseman Dan Uggla), Fernández said he expects big things from his team in the second half of the season.

Three-time All-Star and ESPN commentator Rick Sutcliffe told Fernández before Tuesday's game he was a big fan of his but was disappointed he probably wouldn't get to broadcast one of his games because the Marlins are a last-place team. Fernández politely shook his head and smiled.

"People can think what they want, but I think we're going to play even better in the second half," Fernández said. "It's a different energy. We're hitting the ball well. There isn't a game we play now where we don't think we can win."

Manny Navarro

Friday, July 19, 2013

SHARING THE EXPERIENCE WITH HIS MOTHER

It has been a dreamy rookie season for 20-year-old Marlins rookie José Fernández, one made even sweeter by the All-Star experience he got to share with his mother Maritza in New York earlier this week.

"We actually stayed in the same room, talking until two, three in the morning every night," said Fernández.

"My mom got to do a lot shopping with me [in New York]. I was happy about that."

José Fernández gets a kiss from his mother Maritza after the Marlins defeated the Cleveland Indians 10-0, August 2, 2013. (Pedro Portal/el Nuevo Herald)

Fernández, who said Thursday he answered every text message he received from family, teammates and old friends after his stellar All-Star performance, knows the good times – at least for this season – are not going to last forever. In fact, he's OK with the fact the number of starts he has left this season are numbered.

The Marlins, who open the second half of their season Friday night in Milwaukee, have had their 2011 first-round pick on an innings count all season. And despite the rookie's first-half success, they still plan on shutting him down early to protect his young arm – likely in late August or early September.

"What we said was 150 to 170 innings," Manager Mike Redmond said Thursday, after his team got back together for the first time after the All-Star break for an afternoon practice at Marlins Park. "Obviously we're going to push for closer to 170."

Fernández, who had never pitched above Single A before he surprisingly made the Marlins' Opening Day roster back in April, threw 104 2/3 innings in the first half of the season. Last year, he threw a total of 134 innings between stints with Greensboro (N.C.) and Jupiter.

This first half, he finished 5-5 with a 2.75 ERA, 103 strikeouts and 40 walks. A total of 66 percent of his pitches went for strikes. In all, Fernández has thrown 1,617 pitches – an average of nearly 90 pitches a start. The only time he eclipsed 100 pitches was in four of his last six starts.

Redmond said he never thinks about the long-term innings limit Fernández is on when he takes the mound. He said he goes "solely on how he's doing that day."

"If he has a chance to win a ball game or whatever it is, and he's going good then we'll let him throw seven or eight innings," Redmond said. "I've never gone into a game going we can only let him throw six innings a day. I take it from game to game. If he has a chance to throw a complete game then I'll let him throw a complete game. If he keeps his pitches down and he has a chance he'll go out there."

But protecting Fernández's young arm for the long term is still important to Redmond. Fernández, for his part, would love to pitch the entire season, but he said he has no problem with the Marlins' plans in part because they have been up front since the beginning.

"They know I love to pitch, love to compete. They got a plan and I'm going to follow it 100 percent," Fernández said. "My next start is on Tuesday [in Colorado], and I'm going to go out there and do the best I can until they take me out. The next one after that should be five days after that and I'm going to do the best I can. That's how I'm taking it. I'm not really thinking about innings and stuff like that."

Manny Navarro

MAKING A CASE FOR NL ROOKIE OF THE YEAR

The Marlins have had three players – Dontrelle Willis, Hanley Ramirez and Chris Coghlan – capture National League Rookie of the Year honors.

In José Fernández, they believe they have a fourth in the making.

"I'm biased," Manager Mike Redmond said. "But I think he definitely deserves that honor. I've watched this kid over the course of the year, and I can't imagine there being a better rookie than him. He's been amazing."

A Marlins fan displays a banner supporting José Fernández for Rookie of the Year, September 11, 2013. (José A. Iglesias/el Nuevo Herald)

One day after Fernández struck out 14 Indians, Redmond and the 21-year-old pitcher's teammates were still singing his praises.

Some follow-up tidbits from Friday's performance:

Fernández's 27 combined strikeouts over his past two outings are the most ever in consecutive games by any Marlins pitcher. Ricky Nolasco owned the previous mark with 23.

According to the Elias Sports Bureau, Fernández is just the fifth pitcher under the age of 22 since 1900 to record consecutive games of 13 strikeouts or more. He joined Dennis Eckersley (1976), Dwight Gooden (1984), José Rijo (1986) and Kerry Wood (1998).

Fernández is also the first pitcher with consecutive games of 13 or more whiffs and one or fewer walks since Curt Schilling in 2002.

At the moment, Fernández's chief competition for Rookie of the Year honors appears to be the Dodgers' Yasiel Puig and the Cardinals' Shelby Miller.

Clark Spencer

Chapter 6

PASSION FOR LIFE

José Fernández playing with a sea creature at the 2014 T-Mobile Miami Marlins Winter Warm-Up at Marlins Park, February 15, 2014. (David Santiago/el Nuevo Herald)

Wednesday, August 14, 2013

FREE SPIRIT

José Fernández was dancing when he arrived for work on Tuesday. The 21-year-old rookie entered the Marlins clubhouse at

4 p.m. wearing headphones and grooving to a beat only he could hear.

A couple of his bemused teammates looked up, smiled and shook their heads. It was just Fernández being Fernández, the happiest-go-luckiest free spirit on the club.

On the mound, though, Fernández is all business.

And Tuesday, it was business as usual for the Marlins' young gun as he bolstered his Rookie of the Year candidacy by playing with the Kansas City Royals for seven innings.

Fernández didn't factor in the decision – a 1-0 victory by the Marlins in 10 innings as fellow rookie Christian Yelich drove in the deciding run with a one-out single off Kelvin Herrera.

But it was only fitting that Yelich should come up with the clutch hit, as it was only a bit more than a year ago that he and Fernández showed up together for the Futures Game at Kaufmann Stadium.

"Since the All-Star Game, he's been a different pitcher," manager Mike Redmond said of Fernández. "This guy, confidence-wise, he's going out there going, 'I want to be the best pitcher in the league.' And you know what? He's making a case."

Redmond thought Fernández's changeup on Tuesday was the best it has ever been, and the pitcher agreed.

"It's something I've been working on since spring training," Fernández said. "I threw the first one in the second inning, and I knew it was working. So I wanted to save it a little bit to use it later in the game if I needed it, and that was the case."

It was the seventh 1-0 victory in Marlins history requiring extra innings, and their second 1-0 victory of the road trip. They defeated Atlanta by the same score Saturday.

It was a battle of one of the majors' brightest young stars against one of the league's grizzled veterans, a 21-year-old facing a 36-year-old in Bruce Chen. Chen stood up to the challenge, delivering seven shutout innings in which he held the Marlins to three hits.

Only once during Chen's stay on the mound were the Marlins able to advance a runner past first, and that came in the seventh when Adeiny Hechavarria walked and stole second with two outs. The Marlins squandered their best scoring chance in the ninth, firing a blank after Logan Morrison took second on a sacrifice bunt. Donovan Solano struck out swinging on a ball in the dirt, and Hechavarria grounded to short.

But they finally broke through in the 10th after Jake Marisnick was hit by a pitch to start the inning, stole second and scored on Yelich's single to right.

Yelich went 3 for 4 and had half of the Marlins' six total hits.

"It was a tough night to get hits and score runs for both teams," Yelich said. "I knew if we could just put one across late, we'd have a good chance to win."

The Royals had almost no success against Fernández, failing to put a runner in scoring position until Billy Butler walked and advanced to second on an Alcides Escobar single with two outs in the seventh.

The Marlins received strong bullpen work from Mike Dunn, Chad Qualls and Steve Cishek. Cishek recorded his 25th save.

All told, the Royals managed only four hits off Marlins pitching while losing for only the sixth time – against 19 wins – since the All-Star break.

Fernández added seven more innings to his season count as he approaches the limit of 150 to 170 innings the organization has placed on him. His total now stands at 139 2/3.

But it was another brilliant performance that was brought to a stop after he threw 94 pitches.

Fernández gave up a single in the first inning and another in the second before retiring 13 in a row. He finished the night with six strikeouts and lowered his ERA to 2.45, which ranks fifth in the National League.

Clark Spencer

Wednesday, September 18, 2013

NO *CAMBIES*!

An open letter to Marlins rookie pitching sensation José Fernández:

No *cambies*! Don't change!

Don't tone down. Not even a little. Ignore the purists and the critics. Keep being your exuberant self. Keep leading cheers from the dugout. Keep joking and laughing and engaging in conversations with opposing players. Keep jumping up and down and pumping your fists when your teammates hit home runs. Keep flashing that megawatt smile, the brightest smile around the Marlins clubhouse since another hot-shot rookie pitcher named Dontrelle Willis was making waves with his unorthodox delivery 10 years ago.

José Fernández jokes with Jacob Turner in the dugout in the ninth inning of Marlins vs. Washington Nationals game, won by the Marlins 7-0, September 6, 2013. (Pedro Portal/el Nuevo Herald)

No *cambies*! Don't change!

You felt like taking a second or two to stand at the plate and admire your first career home run as it cleared the fence last week? Who can blame you? You deserve that moment of joy, and then some. You were not disrespecting the Atlanta Braves. You are 21 years old and were celebrating a lifelong dream.

You went to hell and back to reach this country from Cuba. Three times you left your home in Santa Clara and set out on a boat seeking freedom. Three times you wound up back in Cuba, and the third time, at age 14, you were thrown in prison upon your return. You had gotten within view of the twinkling lights of the

Miami skyline on that third attempt, but the Coast Guard intercepted your boat and sent you back. Finally, on the fourth attempt, after having to dive in the water to save your drowning mother, you made it to Mexico, and eventually to Tampa, where the Marlins spotted you.

So, by golly, go ahead and admire that home run. You earned that right. Your courage and persistence should be applauded.

You are the best thing to happen to the Marlins in a long time, and your unbridled affection for your sport is exactly what baseball needs. Athletes in other sports celebrate — and yes, sometimes do look cocky in doing so. Football players break into entertaining end-zone dances after scoring touchdowns. Soccer players around the world celebrate goals with all sorts of creative theatrics. Basketball players wag fingers and showboat. And did anyone around here have more fun while winning than the demonstrative University of Miami Hurricanes of the 1980s? They never hid their joy. They took football seriously, but not at the expense of having fun.

Same goes for Shaquille O'Neal, Charles Barkley, Deion Sanders and the Heat's Chris "The Birdman" Andersen, whose energy and wing-flapping took NBA playoff fun to a whole other level.

It's fun to score. No need to hang your head down and round the bases with no emotion just because that's some kind of unwritten baseball tradition. Despite all its statistics and history, baseball is a game. It's a bunch of guys in funny pants and knee socks who hit and catch a ball and run around a diamond. Be yourself. As long as you're not disrespectful, go for it!

OK, spitting toward the Braves' Chris Johnson while passing third base was out of line. No need for that. But cocky grins from the mound? Taking a moment to soak in a career milestone homer? Go ahead.

"José is an emotional guy, that's part of his game that is going to improve," Marlins Manager Mike Redmond said. "We don't want to take the 'having fun' aspect away from him. That's what makes him him. But at the same time, I think maybe he can center that a little bit. That might be a part of his game he needs to look at, and maybe try to do something different."

Of course, you should respect your manager. Redmond is a good guy who understands that players have different personalities. But when he tells you to "try to do something different," he seems to be saying to tone down, to be more conventional, to harness emotions.

Nah. Disagree.

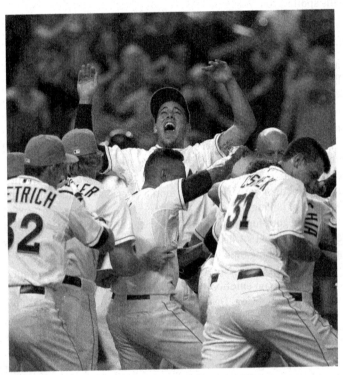

José Fernández celebrates with teammates after right fielder Giancarlo Stanton's walk-off grand slam in the ninth inning of an interleague game against the Seattle Mariners, April 18, 2014. (David Santiago/el Nuevo Herald)

You play for the last-place Marlins, for heaven's sake. There hasn't been much to be excited about all season. You should be applauded for bringing smiles and laughter to that building. You were 9-0 at home with an incredible 1.19 ERA — best in all of baseball. You are a huge reason 25,000 people showed up for that Braves game.

No question you should be named National League Rookie of the Year. Your numbers are sick — 2.19 ERA, second-lowest in the majors behind the Dodgers' Clayton Kershaw. Only three rookie pitchers have done better in the past 65 years. You struck out 187 batters in 172 innings. The Marlins were 18-10 when you started, which means you can be largely thanked for one-third of the team's victories this season.

Five years ago, you were on a boat, bobbing in the rough waters of the Florida Straits, wondering if you'd live or die. Today, you are one of the most entertaining players in Major League Baseball, along with another Cuban defector, Yasiel Puig, who, by the way, has also been asked to tone it down, who has been criticized for over-celebrating and flipping his bat after hitting a home run.

The Cuban passion for baseball is unmatched. It can be infectious. It's good for baseball. Don't let anyone tell you otherwise.

"He's going to be one of the top pitchers in this league for a long time, but you want your players to be judged for the way they compete, not for the theatrics," Redmond said of Fernández.

José, there is nothing wrong with the way you compete. You compete with all your heart and all your soul. Your theatrics make people smile and enjoy a game that too often takes itself too seriously. Here's hoping you'll be remembered for the way you compete, and for your theatrics.

No *cambies*! Don't change!

Michelle Kaufman

Tuesday, November 12, 2013

ROOKIE OF THE YEAR

Willie Mays. Jackie Robinson. Tom Seaver. Pete Rose.

José Fernández added his name to that elite list on Monday when the 21-year-old pitcher for the Marlins was named the National League's Rookie of the Year.

And the best part about it for Fernández was that he was able to enjoy the special moment with perhaps his biggest fan: his 78-year-old grandmother, Olga Fernández Romero.

They embraced after Fernández was told he had won.

"This is out of this world," Fernández said of not only winning the coveted award, but also of having his grandmother on hand to join in the celebration.

Thanks in large part to some behind-the-scenes work by Marlins owner Jeffrey Loria, Fernández Romero received a five-year visitation visa to exit Cuba and visit her grandson in the United States.

To the pitcher's surprise, they were reunited Sunday at Marlins Park.

Fernández became the third Cuban-born player to win a Rookie of the Year award, joining Tony Oliva (1964) and José Canseco (1986). And Fernández had to beat out another Cuban, Dodgers outfielder Yasiel Puig, to claim the title.

Fernández received 26 of 30 first-place votes from members of the Baseball Writers' Association of America, with Puig receiving the other four. The Cardinals' Shelby Miller was third in the voting.

Fernández went 12-6 with a 2.19 ERA that ranked second in the majors. Every fifth day when he took the mound, he helped make a dreadful season for the last-place Marlins a touch more bearable.

Fernández became the fourth Marlin to win the prestigious award for rookies, joining Dontrelle Willis, Hanley Ramirez and Chris Coghlan. He is also the first pitcher from a 100-loss team to win the award since Tom Seaver of the New York Mets in 1967.

The Marlins went 18-10 in games he started.

But Fernández wasn't exceptional only by rookie standards. His season ranked as one of the best among all major-league pitchers — rookie or veteran. As a result, he is also one of three finalists, along with Clayton Kershaw and Adam Wainwright, for the NL Cy Young Award, given to the league's top pitcher.

"I'm happy," Fernández said of his initial success in the majors. "But I think I can get a lot better than I did."

Though the Marlins drafted him with their first-round pick in 2011 out of Tampa's Alonso High, it was still a rapid ascension to stardom for the unflappable right-hander. He was expected to start the season at Double A Jacksonville. But he landed a spot on the Opening Day roster when injuries created a vacancy in the starting rotation.

2013 National League Rookie of the Year José Fernández talks to the media, February 15, 2014. (Pedro Portal/el Nuevo Herald)

Fernández had his ups and downs in April, finishing the month with a 0-2 record. But he took off after that, and from June 1 forward evolved into one of the most dominant pitchers in the majors.

He was picked to represent the Marlins in the All-Star Game, where he retired the three batters he faced, striking out two of them. His dominance didn't end there as he went 7-1 with a 1.32 ERA after the All-Star break.

For the season, opposing batters hit just .182 off Fernández — the best figure for any starting pitcher in the majors. The Texas Rangers' Yu Darvish was next on the list with a batting average against of .194.

"I think next year is going to be a lot harder than my first year," Fernández said. "I haven't touched a ball [since the season ended], but I can't wait to. I can't wait for game time."

Fernández, who defected from Cuba when he was 15, is excited at the prospect of his grandmother finally getting a chance to see him pitch in person next season. She probably won't have to wait long for the opportunity, as he will likely be the Marlins' Opening Day starter on March 31.

"She will come to all my games," he said. "She will fight with umpires. She will do everything. Just having her here and being with her every second of the day is pretty amazing."

Wil Meyers of the Tampa Bay Rays won the American League's Rookie of the Year award.

Clark Spencer

Wednesday, February 12, 2014

MOUND ANTICS

Marlins pitcher José Fernández not only dominated the competition in winning National League Rookie of the Year, but also he had a blast doing it – chit-chatting with opponents during games or grinning after striking them out, to the annoyance of some of those opponents.

Fernández has said he has no intention of changing, but a few Marlins people wonder whether he should curtail his playful exchanges with opponents during games.

"I wouldn't want to see that because you are sending mixed messages," Marlins special assistant Andre Dawson said. "I played in an era you couldn't do that. I would like to see the concentration level different. I like to see more intensity on the mound like, 'I'm here to stick it up your rear end.' [But] he's a good kid. He'll learn. You can't fault him for animation."

In a conversation at the end of last season, Marlins infielder Greg Dobbs expressed some concern about Fernández's theatrics but did not want to chastise him.

"You never want to come across to teammates and opponents as being pompous or grandstanding or insulting," Dobbs said. "I'm not saying those are his intentions. But you don't want to give that perception. We're not here to grandstand or boast."

He said the "best pitchers do not" talk to batters during at-bats.

José Fernández jokes around on the mound against the Atlanta Braves, September 11, 2013. (Pedro Portal/el Nuevo Herald)

"Mariano Rivera doesn't do that," Dobbs said. "You don't need to do that. You can draw extra criticism. You have to put a governor on that excitability. You don't want that to distract."

Dobbs said if it ever "gets to the point where it's a detriment, it would have to be addressed" with him.

Fernández's theatrics led to an incident in September against Atlanta. Annoyed by Evan Gattis' reaction to a home run off him, Fernández screamed at the Braves' dugout.

After Fernández hit a home run during the bottom half of that sixth inning, he admired it and spat on third base. Fernández apologized afterward.

"He's a playful guy on the mound, and he likes to have fun," Braves Manager Fredi Gonzalez said. "... Then he shouldn't get upset when we hit a home run and have fun ourselves. ... You can't have it both ways."

Braves third baseman Chris Johnson said Fernández irritates opponents by grinning after getting them out.

Fernández and Marlins Manager Mike Redmond have said they don't believe Fernández needs to change his on-field demeanor.

"That's how I am," Fernández said late last season. "I like to have fun. I can't be someone I'm not. [Hall of Fame pitcher] Don Sutton told me, 'Don't change. Be who you are.'"

And what about opponents who have a problem with that?

"They're not on my team," he said.

The view here: We have no problem with Fernández engaging opposing players in playful banter, as long as he doesn't cross the line like he did against Atlanta.

Fernández told MLB.com that he biked 70 to 80 miles a day five or six times a week during the offseason and has lost 20 pounds.

Barry Jackson

Tuesday, April 1, 2014

ABUELA AND MAMA

We expect sports' greatest moments to be big and loud, the spectacular plays that splash across live television and lift fans onto their feet. But sometimes the very best moments are small and quiet. They feel private, like snapshots from a family album.

This happened a little more than two hours before the Marlins' season-opening baseball game here Monday night, as the home team took batting practice and the downtown ballpark was just beginning to slowly fill.

José Fernández emerged from the clubhouse carrying two bright orange jerseys both bearing his number 16. On the back of one was stitched the word, ABUELA. The back of the other read, MAMA.

The Marlins' young, star pitcher crept up behind his grandmother and mother, who stood near the wall behind home plate, to present his small gifts from the heart.

José Fernández's grandmother puts on her new Marlins shirt, March 31, 2014. (Hector Gabino/el Nuevo Herald)

Fernández traveled 90 miles and a lifetime to get to where he is today, and will tell you he wouldn't have made it without the love and maternal strength given him.

Monday, his beloved grandmother, his *abuela*, watched him pitch in the big leagues for the first time.

Special jerseys. Special delivery. Special women. Special night.

The Marlins clobbered the Colorado Rockies 10-1 and in storybook fashion favorite son José was the star of the night with nine strikeouts and zero walks in six efficient, nearly unblemished innings. (Amazing what a lot of talent plus a little adrenaline can do.) Marcell Ozuna's solo home run and Casey McGehee's three-run double were the biggest strokes in a 14-hit onslaught — offense that one season ago was all but unheard of.

This was Opening Night, but it was José's night. Rather, his Abuela's.

"I'm very emotional tonight, but that's understandable, no?" said the grandmother, Olga, in Spanish.

She wiped at a tear that slid down her right cheek.

"I just want him to win and wish him lots of luck," she said. "I just hope he's happy. I have so many memories of watching him pitch as a kid."

So does José.

"She'd yell at the umpires," he said, smiling. "That was a strike!"

She didn't have to yell much Monday.

Twenty-four of her grandson's first 27 pitches were strikes. He had at least one strikeout in every inning he pitched.

The franchise's 22nd season and third at Marlins Park opened like a fan's dream. Everything was right. The stadium roof opened to a balmy night. Red, white and blue bunting decorated the park. Dolphins legend Dan Marino threw out the ceremonial first pitch (after which Colorado's Troy Tulowitzki asked Marino to pose for a photograph).

Opening Day "is how I remember feeling as a kid on Christmas Eve," described McGehee, the new Marlins third baseman.

"The plate's clean," said second baseman Jeff Baker. "Everything is fresh."

Even the festive crowd was right, an announced 37,116 that wasn't quite the full house claimed but made merry noise like one.

On Opening Night hope springs eternal, and it does most nights when a certain young pitcher takes the mound for Miami.

José defected from Cuba in 2008 on his fourth attempt, along with his mother Maritza and sister, who settled in Tampa. Olga, here on a visitation visa, had reunited with José last November after six years apart, arranged with the Marlins' help, but hadn't seen him pitch here 'til Monday.

The women sat 10 rows up behind the home dugout, standing to cheer all of José's strikeouts. They were standing a lot.

"I wish him the best always but tonight even more because my mother is going to get the chance to watch him and she hasn't for many years," José's mother had said. "I'm relaxed because I already watched him last year, but she hasn't so she's not calm. It's been such a sudden change in his life. It hasn't given us time to really realize everything he's done."

Fernández was NL Rookie of the Year last season and second in voting for the Cy Young award. Now at 21 he has become the youngest Marlins Opening Day starter, youngest in MLB since 2007, and youngest in the NL since Dwight Gooden, who was 20, in 1985.

That Fernández is such a quintessential Miami story gives him a chance to grow to become a home-grown (team-drafted) star close to the level Marino was to the Dolphins and what Dwyane Wade was to the Heat. He is that special.

A joking teammate hung a jersey in Fernández's locker Monday that intentionally misspelled his name and had the wrong number. The prank was unnecessary, of course.

Keeping José grounded seems to be in safe hands with the women he calls Mama and Abuela.

Greg Cote

Chapter 7

GOLDEN ARM

José Fernández in the first inning of the Marlins vs. San Diego Padres game, Marlins Park, April 5, 2014. (Pedro Portal/el Nuevo Herald)

Tuesday, April 1, 2014

BRINGING OUT THE BEST IN THE MARLINS

So starved for runs were Marlins pitchers a season ago that nobody would have faulted them had they stood at home plate, shaking tin cups and begging for handouts.

They lived off crumbs.

Maybe times have changed.

Before a sellout crowd of 37,116 that was announced as the largest in Marlins Park history, and on the opening night of a new season, the reconfigured lineup showed life, providing pitcher José Fernández with support the likes of which Marlins pitchers seldom experienced in 2013.

The result: a 10-1 victory over the Colorado Rockies.

Fernández did his usual thing, fanning nine to match Josh Beckett's 2004 record for most strikeouts by a Marlins pitcher in a season opener while hanging around for only six innings.

"I was really not trying to throw 100 miles per hour," said Fernández, who tried to contain his adrenalin for the outing.

But it was the offense — and the bottom of the order, in particular — that showed surprising spark.

Marcell Ozuna, he who was outplayed all spring by Jake Marisnick, suddenly came to life on the first day that games counted, going 3 for 4 with a single, double and home run. And eighth hitter Adeiny Hechavarria, who had not played in a week due to a tight groin, also had three hits.

The big inning for the Marlins came in the fifth when they erupted for five runs off Rockies starter Jorge De La Rosa, with newcomer Casey McGehee driving in three with a bases-loaded double.

To put that into some context, five runs was the most scored in any one inning last season by the Marlins. The Marlins also went their first four games last season before anyone on the team drove in a run with a runner in scoring position.

But after Ozuna doubled in the fifth, Hechavarria drove him in with the first of his three base hits.

Ozuna acknowledged that he was "worried" he wouldn't make the team after hitting just .177 this spring while Marisnick hit over .400.

"But they gave me an opportunity," he said. "Now I need to grab it and put it in my pocket."

Those two weren't the only ones doing damage.

Giancarlo Stanton drove in a pair of runs, one coming on a squib single and the other on a double over the head of Rockies right fielder Michael Cuddyer. The Marlins pounded out 13 hits total.

It was more than enough for Fernández, who coasted Monday.

Fernández pounded the strike zone, challenging the Rockies to take their cuts. Of his 94 total pitches, 74 were strikes.

Fernández's grandmother, Olga, was on hand to see her grandson pitch for the first time since he was 14 and still living in Cuba.

"You did good, but you've got to throw a lot more strikes," she told him afterward.

And the Rockies took their hacks, swinging early and often.

Of the 27 pitches thrown by Fernández in the first two innings, 23 were swung at by the Rockies. He retired 10 in a row from the first to the fourth, with seven of those outs coming on strikeouts.

Catcher Jarrod Saltalamacchia said the Rockies' strategy was obvious.

"They didn't want to get to his slider," Saltalamacchia said. "They wanted to get to him before he got to them."

Fernández was unyielding until the sixth when Carlos Gonzalez crushed a solo home run to center, which the Rockies slugger stood and admired.

Fernández, looking a bit gassed, was lifted after the sixth. But he earned the win to improve to 10-0 in his career at Marlins Park.

Clark Spencer

Tuesday, May 13, 2014

TOMMY JOHN SURGERY

José Fernández is expected to undergo Tommy John surgery — perhaps within days — after a second doctor confirmed the diagnosis of the first: a torn ulnar collateral ligament in his right elbow, sources said.

Fernández was examined in Miami on Tuesday by Dr. Lee Kaplan, the Marlins' team physician, one day after being examined by another doctor in Los Angeles.

Marlins President of Baseball Operations Michael Hill termed the tear as "significant" and that "Tommy John surgery has been recommended."

"Obviously a lot has gone on the past few days, a lot for him to take in, a lot to absorb, so he is taking the time digesting all the information he has been given from both doctors," Hill said. "The sooner we can get a decision the sooner we can get surgery set up."

Hill said it has not yet been decided who will perform the surgery.

"From what our doctors saw, they did not want to go the rehab [nonsurgical] route," Hill said. "They felt surgery was the best option."

The earliest Fernández can be expected to return to the mound from elbow ligament replacement surgery is 12 months, and it could take as long as 18 months before he's back on the mound for the Marlins.

"We're hopeful he'll come back and be better than ever and be comparable to the José we've seen perform in the last year," Hill said.

Hill noted that former Marlins pitcher Josh Johnson returned in 11 months from Tommy John surgery, but cautioned that every pitcher is different.

Fernández complained of discomfort in his elbow after pitching Friday in San Diego.

Marlins Manager Mike Redmond said Tuesday it's difficult to know what caused Fernández's injury, or why there has been a sudden rash of elbow injuries requiring Tommy John surgery.

"I don't think anybody has a true answer of why," Redmond said. "I wish we could find a reason for it because it's sad. I wish we could figure out a way to keep these guys on the field."

The Marlins did everything they could to protect Fernández's valuable arm outside of surrounding him in bubble wrap and packing peanuts:

- They capped his innings in the minors.
- They shut him down in mid-September of his rookie season.
- They never allowed him to pitch the ninth inning, ever-mindful of his pitch count.

And yet, despite all that, the 21-year-old hurler still sustained a serious arm injury after making only 36 big-league starts, eight of them coming this season.

Fernández, who was the National League's Rookie of the Year last season and finished third in Cy Young Award voting, lost velocity on his fastball during Friday's outing in San Diego.

"You're never going to replace him, but someone's going to have to step up," Hill said.

Hill said the organization took all the necessary steps with Fernández to prevent an arm injury. But there is never a guarantee.

"We've been protective throughout the minor leagues with all of our starting pitchers," Hill said. "We try to protect them as best we can and build them up when we get to the big leagues, and get them ready for what they're facing."

The Marlins are calling up Anthony DeSclafani to take Fernández's spot in the rotation. DeSclafani, 24, will make his major-league debut Wednesday against the Dodgers.

Scott Boras, Fernández's agent, said pitchers with "huge engines" like the Marlins' ace are more susceptible to injuries. Boras cited two of his other clients — Matt Harvey and Stephen Strasburg — as other examples. Harvey and Strasburg have each had Tommy John surgery.

"[They] have the ability to do things beyond the levels of your durability because their talent is so high," Boras said. "A veteran pitcher knows the boundaries of that. They have the big engines. They also have the steering wheel of experience to go with it."

Clark Spencer

Wednesday, May 14, 2014

FLAME THROWING TAKES ITS TOLL

The Marlins took every precautionary measure they could to protect José Fernández's golden arm short of storing his elbow in a safe or hiring a bodyguard to lift his fork to his lips at mealtimes.

They counted his pitches the way a miser counts coins. They gave him the kind of rest even a baby would envy. They put him on early vacation three weeks before the season ended in 2013.

José Fernández pitches in the second inning against the Los Angeles Dodgers, May 4, 2014. (David Santiago/el Nuevo Herald)

Didn't matter. The one thing the Marlins could not do — nor could Fernández — was force him to ease up on his pitches. Throw with less velocity. Take a little off the fastball that gives hitters whiplash. Reduce power on the slider that makes wicked detours at the plate.

Fernández didn't win National League Rookie of the Year or toss more strikeouts than any other pitcher so far this season (70) by being conservative on the mound.

But his right elbow couldn't take it anymore. Fernández fears an awful diagnosis: A tear in the ulnar collateral ligament that will require Tommy John surgery, 12-18 months of rehabilitation, the end of this season and erasure of half the next.

Just when the Marlins were winning games and creating a buzz, down goes their dynamic ace. Just when Fernández was proving to be a must-see magnet at Marlins Park, where he is 12-0 and drew more than 30,000 for his last start, and nationwide, where he leads the majors in limiting opponents to a .183 batting average, his career goes on hiatus.

Bad karma for a franchise burdened by so much ill will, not to mention the 100 losses last season? Bad luck for Fernández? Or simply inevitable, given the epidemic in baseball these days? If Fernández, 21, opts for Tommy John surgery, he will be the 33rd player to undergo the procedure in the past year. Since January, 22 pitchers have had the operation. Two of the top draft prospects have had the surgery in the past week.

Football players blow out knees, which is not surprising given the collision of a violent game with bigger, stronger athletes. Pitchers, even coddled ones, are blowing out elbows at an alarming rate. They, too, are bigger and stronger than they used to be, and they are subjecting the human anatomy to forces it was not designed to withstand.

Tommy John was 31 and a 12-year veteran when he became the first pitcher to undergo the ligament replacement surgery in 1974, performed by orthopedic pioneer Dr. Frank Jobe. In recent years, the average age of pitchers requiring the surgery has plunged. They are feeling the effects of throwing too hard, too often from a young age. Go watch a high school game. Top teens are throwing 95 mph pitches. They are also playing year-round.

Fernández will join a list that includes Matt Harvey, Matt Moore, Kris Medlen, Patrick Corbin and Brandon Beachy. Former Marlins ace Josh Johnson, who had the surgery in 2007, had it for a second time this spring. So did Jarrod Parker, five years after he had his first elbow reconstruction.

Baseball has a problem. Its young pitchers throw so hard that strikeouts are up for the ninth season in a row, with the concurrent trend that those pitchers break down. Pitch and six-inning limits can't go much lower lest teams have to add more relievers to the roster and resort to more tiresome pitching changes in games. Youth-league coaches and parents must be vigilant about controlling pitchers' workload, and baseball at all levels, including MLB, should consider the suggestion to lower the pitcher's mound, which would reduce arm strain and pitch speed.

Like Steve Austin, the Six Million Dollar Man, Fernández can be rebuilt to come back better than he was before — although Jobe said pitchers came back as good as they were before, but with more attention to fitness. John pitched another 14 years post-rehab, and the success rate of the surgery has climbed to better than 85 percent since then.

But the Marlins still lose a year of Fernández's career. They have won 64 percent of his starts compared to 36 percent with their other starters. Even if they weren't expected to have a stellar season, they have been a pleasant surprise, even flirting with first place, and his absence early next season will truly hurt their progress. Hear the clock ticking on Giancarlo Stanton's days as a Marlin? He has to be very disappointed in this turn of events.

Fernández was placed on the disabled list three days after his pitch speed dropped to 90.7 mph in the last two innings of a poor outing in San Diego.

His dramatic escape from Cuba, unabashed devotion to his grandmother and exuberant nature make him the perfect star for Miami's much-maligned baseball team. He will return, but it could be a long wait to see the 97-mph fastball that was his asset, and his undoing.

Linda Robertson

Chapter 8

BECOMING A U.S. CITIZEN

José Fernández proudly waves an American flag after becoming a U.S. citizen, April 24, 2015. (José A. Iglesias/el Nuevo Herald)

Saturday, April 25, 2015

PROUD TO BE AN AMERICAN

Marlins pitcher José Fernández ditched his team colors on Friday for the red, white and blue of his adopted nation.

Donning a dark suit and wearing his hair slicked back, the 22-year-old waved a miniature American flag to Lee Greenwood's "I'm Proud to be an American" song, as he joined 140 other South Florida residents in becoming U.S. citizens.

During the ceremony, Cuban-born Fernández, along with the other applicants, took an oath of allegiance at the U.S. Citizenship and Immigration Services Kendall field office.

A nervous Fernández addressed the room of new citizens, who originated from Vietnam, Venezuela and 20 countries in between, during a keynote speech.

"I respect everyone who makes this country what it is today and I don't think we should take that for granted," he said. "It is an honor to be a U.S. citizen and that's all I've got to say."

For the youngest Marlins Opening Day starter, becoming a U.S. citizen was one of his dreams from a young age. "I feel respect for those people who defend our country, for the people that go out there and risk their lives every day for us," he said. "You want to be free, and that's what it's all about today."

Fernández defected to the United States in 2008 on his fourth attempt from his hometown of Santa Clara, Cuba. Settling in Tampa, he attended Alonso High, where the Marlins drafted him with their first-round pick in 2011. After spending two seasons in the minor leagues, he made his MLB debut in 2013, the same year that he won the NL Rookie of the Year title.

Ariel Rodríguez, a 20-year-old Marlins fan who aspires to become an air-traffic controller or a pilot, also defected from Cuba five years ago.

José Fernández becomes a U.S. citizen, April 24, 2015. (José A. Iglesias/el Nuevo Herald)

"I am proud to be a U.S. citizen. This is a great country," he said.

The Marlins honored the new citizens with two tickets to attend any two games during this season.

For fans, Fernández is expected to be back on the mound this summer. He hasn't pitched a game since last May after an elbow injury that required Tommy John surgery.

"I thank this amazing country for giving me the opportunity to go to school here, learn the language and pitch in the major leagues," Fernández said. "It's an honor to be a part of this country, and I respect it so much."

Kathleen Devaney

Wednesday, March 23, 2016

'IT'S A DREAM TO COME TO AMERICA AND PLAY BASEBALL'

José Fernández is very interested in the Tampa Bay Rays' exhibition game against the Cuban national team Tuesday afternoon in Havana.

Fernández, the Marlins' 23-year old, Cuban-born ace, tried to escape his home country multiple times until he finally did successfully on his fourth try in 2008 — a journey that nearly cost his mother her life.

So while he sees it as an opportunity for the people of his native land to watch American professional baseball up close, Fernández feels plenty still needs to change for it to have a true impact.

"Hopefully this is the beginning of change over there," Fernández said. "We all have our concerns about what is going on there. It gives you some hope when things like this happen and you see the president [of the United States] over there now.

"But a lot still has to change."

Fernández, who was born in Santa Clara, Cuba, fled the island when he was 15 years old with his mother and sister.

After three failed attempts, he served prison time for being a dissident.

Fernández and his family finally made it to Tampa, where he was reunited with his stepfather. But on the way across the turbulent waters of the Gulf of Mexico to Mexico, Fernández's mother nearly drowned after she fell overboard, but he jumped in and saved her life.

Although much has been made of the baseball impact of the game, Fernández doesn't think it will bring enough attention to the plight of the Cuban people under the communist regime.

"I think the players [from the U.S.] that go to Cuba will see a lot of reality," Fernández said. "They will see a lot of things that we take for granted here that people over there don't. Pretty much over there, people don't have anything.

"But they're probably not going to go inside the cities and see the real life and real struggles of the people over there."

Fernández enrolled at Alonso High in Tampa and began his journey to major-league stardom.

U.S. citizen, José Fernández, April 24, 2015. (José A. Iglesias/el Nuevo Herald)

The Marlins drafted him out of high school in 2011 and he made his debut in 2013, later becoming the National League's Rookie of the Year and finishing third in the Cy Young Award voting that season.

Fernández also became a U.S. citizen last year in April.

"For all of us, it's a dream to come to America and play baseball," Fernández said. "Some of us will do whatever it takes to achieve that. Hopefully, this will open a lot of doors and can change a lot of things."

Fernández said that from a baseball standpoint, the game will benefit the people of Cuba and many young players like him dreaming of playing in the major leagues — many of whom will get to see a MLB team up close for the first time.

But Fernández showed mixed emotions when asked if he would like to see the Marlins play a game in Cuba someday or if he would ever consider playing for the Cuban national team if the political situation changed.

"My grandmother would love to see me pitch over there," Fernández said. "It would be a dream for her, but I would only do it under the right circumstances. There's really not one thing I can point out that needs to change. I could go over all of them, but I'd be here all day and I have to pitch today.

"So many things would need to change before I would ever do that. I went through so many things and my family went through so much to get here, that a lot would have to change."

Andre C. Fernandez

Chapter 9

THE 2016 SEASON

José Fernández after the Marlins' 1-0 victory against the New York Mets at Marlins Park, June 5, 2016. (Pedro Portal/el Nuevo Herald)

GROWING AS A PITCHER

Friday, May 27, 2016

A WIN AT TROPICANA FIELD, FINALLY

The names on the Marlins' lineup card looked as though they had either been pulled randomly from a hat or were the manifestation of a manager gone mad.

Had Don Mattingly lost his mind?

There was Adeiny Hechavarria in the leadoff spot.

There was J.T. Realmuto batting cleanup.

Given the Marlins' 9-1 victory over the Tampa Bay Rays on Thursday afternoon, perhaps it was the work of genius.

With Giancarlo Stanton and Christian Yelich out with injuries and a left-hander on the mound for the Rays, Mattingly got creative and scribbled down nine names he thought would give the depleted Marlins their best shot at winning.

It worked.

A re-configured lineup that contained a generous helping of reserves produced a satisfying win for the Marlins, who took the Citrus Series three games to one.

Toss in another dominating start by José Fernández and the result was a victory that kept the Marlins (25-22) in the thick of a four-team logjam in the National League East. Now they head off to Atlanta to face the last-place Braves, who swept them in April in Miami but have gone 2-19 at Turner Field.

Fernández won for the first time in three tries at Tropicana Field, where he watched his first major-league game after defecting from Cuba. He finished with a dozen strikeouts over seven innings and tied Ricky Nolasco on the team's all-time list for most career 10-strikeout games with 13.

"I think this is a tough place for him, just because of the emotion of Tampa and the whole thing," Mattingly said. "This is a place where he kind of has to pull the reins off a little bit."

Fernández was dealt with distractions aplenty on Thursday.

First, the Rays' mascot was messing with him during his pregame warmups in the bullpen.

Mildly irked, Fernández plunked the mascot with a changeup.

"The ball was slippery," Fernández said with a smile. "He was all over my business, and I'm trying to concentrate. This is a game, and I love to have fun. [But] he was too close. I've never seen that. I'm like, 'Guy, I think you need to move.'"

Then, after working out of a bases-loaded jam in the fourth by retiring Curt Casali on a foul pop, Fernández reacted visibly, and it apparently irked some in the Rays dugout.

"It was a tough situation for me," Fernández said of the bases-loaded situation. "I showed some emotion. I was like, 'Yeah,' and I was really happy to get out of it. I heard something from the [Rays] dugout. Didn't pay much attention to it."

Fernández got the last laugh. From the fifth through the seventh, he struck out eight Rays, including all three batters he faced in his final inning.

But it was Mattingly's odd lineup, something that one is more likely to see in spring training than during the regular season, that came through for the Marlins.

After reserve infielder Miguel Rojas put the Marlins on top in the second by punctuating his 10-pitch at-bat with an RBI single, Hechavarria slammed a two-run homer off Rays starter Drew Smyly.

One inning later, reserve first baseman Chris Johnson also connected on a two-run homer, and Fernández and the Marlins made it hold up.

Johnson banged out another RBI hit in the eighth, and Cole Gillespie, who was filling in for Stanton, added RBI hits in the eighth and ninth innings.

Fernández, who the Marlins drafted out of Tampa's Alonso High in 2011, pitched poorly in his previous two starts in front of friends and family members at Tropicana, losing both times.

That wasn't the case on Thursday.

Other than a solo homer he gave up to Brandon Guyer in the third and that shaky fourth inning in which the Rays loaded the bases on him after two were out, Fernández dazzled in front of his vocal following. He exited after totaling 111 pitches in those seven innings.

Clark Spencer

Saturday, June 11, 2016

PITCHING BETTER THAN EVER

José Fernández is no longer out to show the world that his surgically repaired arm is healthy, or that every fastball he delivers must be thrown at maximum velocity, which is why he thinks he's pitching better than ever before.

Call it a change of mind-set.

"I'm not trying to prove to everyone that I'm healthy and that I'm back," said Fernández, who, two years removed from Tommy John surgery, will be taking aim on a Marlins franchise record on

Saturday when he faces the Diamondbacks. "I felt I had to go the extra mile when all I had to do was pitch."

With wins in each of his past eight starts, Fernández is tied with Chris Hammond for the team record. Incredibly, Hammond won eight consecutive starts for the 1993 Marlins, an expansion team that finished 64-98.

"I'm not here to break records," Fernández said. "I'm here to win ballgames and give us a good chance to win."

Since starting the season 1-2, Fernández has done just that, going 8-0 with a 1.38 ERA. He is tied for the major-league lead with nine wins and his strikeout rate of 13.3 whiffs per nine innings leads the majors.

"He's pitching like a pitcher," Manager Don Mattingly said. "I think we see a more under control guy who is using his whole mix and not just trying to throw the ball through the wall every pitch."

Mattingly said he has detected a couple of changes in Fernández since April.

For one, Mattingly said Fernández is changing speeds on his fastball, "being able to use a 92 [mph] fastball and then go to 96 or 97. It's like having two different fastballs instead of just using one."

For another, Fernández has learned to temper his nervous energy.

"I think he's emotional, that hasn't changed," Mattingly said. "But I think he's been more calm before his starts."

Mattingly cited an example involving Fernández near the start of the season.

"The one game I remember, he hit for like an hour before the game," Mattingly said. "He just said he was bored and he had to do something. And then it seemed like he was tired during the game. [Now], I think he's stayed a little calmer before the games, saving his energy."

Though he's taken some of the steam off his fastball by design, Fernández is still getting his high share of strikeouts. In his most recent start, Fernández whiffed 14 New York Mets to equal a career high.

"Strikeouts are great," Fernández said. "They're fun and everybody loves them. But I'm not looking for them. I'm not looking for strikeouts. I'm looking for quick outs. I'm growing."

Clark Spencer

Monday, June 13, 2016

TURNING INTO A PUMPKIN

José Fernández was 10 outs from perfection, at which point he suddenly turned into a pumpkin.

Fernández, who had retired the first 17 batters on Saturday night, suddenly imploded in a seismic sixth inning against Arizona.

Michael Bourn, who had not homered in nearly two years, broke up his no-hit bid with a two-out solo shot in the sixth, and Fernández gave up hits to the next four Arizona hitters as the Diamondbacks rallied for a 5-3 victory.

"That's the funny thing about baseball, that anybody at any point can do damage," Fernández said. "That's the beauty of [baseball]. You've got to stay on your toes all the time."

It was Fernández's first loss since April 23, ending an eight-game win streak.

"He was cruising," Manager Don Mattingly said. "It just kind of came apart there. Usually, with José, nothing really bothers him. He just continues on. But it just kind of got away from him there."

Fernández had gone 23 consecutive innings without allowing a run before the Diamondbacks erupted for four runs off him in the sixth on Saturday.

Clark Spencer

Sunday, July 3, 2016

PINCH HITTER

José Fernández wanted to stay up past bedtime and play with the boys.

Good thing for the Marlins he did.

Fernández drove in the go-ahead runs in a 7-5 Marlins victory with his pinch-hit double in the 12th inning on Friday night.

"It's always been like a dream to play the outfield or pinch-hit like that," Fernández said. "But when it actually happened I was [like], 'Oh, my gosh. I shouldn't be doing this.' My heart really started going faster."

Marlins Manager Don Mattingly had exhausted his bench by the time he turned to Fernández – the team's best hitting pitcher – to grab a bat in the 12th.

Because he was scheduled to start on Saturday afternoon, Fernández had been advised earlier Friday to return to the hotel and rest. But Fernández wanted no part of that.

"As the game unfolded, he kind of wanted to stay," Mattingly said.

Fernández joined Dennis Cook as the only pitchers in Marlins history to deliver game-winning pinch-hits.

It was the 11th pinch-hit by a Marlins pitcher. Six of those belong to Dontrelle Willis.

Clark Spencer

Sunday, July 3, 2016

SHOULD HAVE GOTTEN A GOOD NIGHT'S SLEEP

Maybe José Fernández should have gotten that good night's sleep after all.

One day after driving in the winning runs in a pinch-hitting cameo, Fernández was roughed up by the last-place Atlanta Braves in the worst outing of his career. Fernández gave up all nine runs in a 9-1 battering by the Braves on Saturday.

"Rough day, man," Fernández said.

It was another dumbfounding defeat to a Braves team that would be running away with the National League East if only they could play the Marlins in all 162 games. They are 8-3 against the Marlins this year, 20-50 against everyone else.

Even with Fernández on the mound in an obvious mismatch against a Braves starter – Lucas Harrell – who last pitched in the majors two years ago, the Marlins still couldn't find a way to win.

They mustered only three hits in six innings against Harrell.

"It's called baseball. Baseball doesn't make much sense," said Fernández, whose record fell to 10-4.

Said Marlins Manager Don Mattingly: "I thought [Harrell] carved us up pretty good, honestly. We didn't do much with him."

Their only bright spot at the plate came in the third when Ichiro Suzuki drove in the Marlins' only run with a triple. The hit pushed Ichiro's career total to 2,989, leaving him 11 shy of 3,000.

But the Braves made easing pickings of Fernández, jumping out to a lead on Freddie Freeman's two-run homer in the first before unloading on him in a seven-run sixth.

"I thought he was throwing the ball pretty good," Mattingly said. "It wasn't a typical José, but I thought he threw the ball good enough. I feel like if we had come out and swung the bats a little better for him, it's probably a different game. He's just trying to hang in there, keep it 2-1. It puts a lot of pressure on him to do that."

Three of the runs that Fernández allowed were unearned because of a Chris Johnson error. Nonetheless, the Braves batted around against Fernández in the sixth, lashing out with five hits, including a three-run homer by Jace Peterson that sent him to the showers.

"This game is hard," Fernández said. "It's not easy. It's not easy at all. They've got a tough lineup. They're playing good baseball. It won't be the last time it's going to happen. Hopefully, it doesn't happen that often."

Fernández simply ran out of gas.

During Friday night's long game, coaches suggested to Fernández that he return to the team hotel and rest up for Saturday's start. But he elected to stick around for the 12-inning affair and won the game with his bat.

In an unfathomable role reversal, he lost Saturday's game with his arm.

"I'm sure that is emotional to do something like that," Mattingly said of Fernández's hitting heroics the night before. "I know he's an emotional kid and probably had a little trouble sleeping. It could have had something to do with it."

But Fernández said he got "normal" sleep.

"I don't think [Friday night] has to do with anything with the results [Saturday]," Fernández said. "I felt I was throwing the ball well. They played better, that simple."

Clark Spencer

2016 MOMENTS

José Fernández pitches in the first inning against the Pittsburgh Pirates, May 31, 2016. (Pedro Portal/el Nuevo Herald)

José Fernández greets closer A.J. Ramos after he finishes the ninth inning for a victory against the Pittsburgh Pirates, May 31, 2016. (Pedro Portal/el Nuevo Herald)

Marlins pitchers Wei-Yin Chen, left, and José Fernández react as closer
A.J. Ramos gets the last out in a 1-0 victory against the Mets, June 5,
2016. (Pedro Portal/al Nuevo Herald)

Fernández singles for the first run against Atlanta in the second inning,
June 21, 2016. (Pedro Portal/Miami Herald)

José Fernández hits a sacrifice bunt in the fifth inning against the Mets, July 23, 2016. (Pedro Portal/el Nuevo Herald)

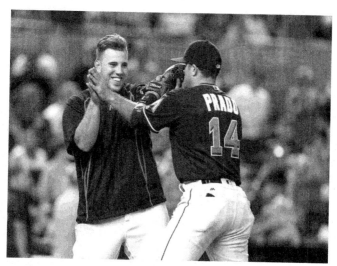

José Fernández and third baseman Martin Prado celebrate their 6-2 victory against the Mets, July 23, 2016. (Pedro Portal/el Nuevo Herald)

José Fernández reacts after reaching first base on an infield single in the third inning of the Marlins-Royals game, August 24, 2016. (Pedro Portal/el Nuevo Herald)

Marlins player Miguel Rojas smashes a plate of shaving cream into José Fernández's face in celebration of their 3-0 victory over the Kansas City Royals, August 24, 2016. (Pedro Portal/el Nuevo Herald)

José Fernández and David Phelps celebrate the Marlins' 1-0 victory over Washington Nationals, September 20, 2016. (Pedro Portal/el Nuevo Herald)

Marlins hitting coach Barry Bonds greets José Fernández as they celebrate the Marlins victory, September 20, 2016. (Pedro Portal/Miami Herald)

ALL-STAR AGAIN

JOSÉ FERNÁNDEZ
ALL-STAR GAME STATISTICS

YEAR	W	L	ERA	SV	IP	H	R	ER	HR	BB	SO
2013	0	0	0.00	0	1.0	0	0	0	0	0	2
2016	0	0	6.75	0	1.1	2	1	1	0	1	1
Totals	0	0	3.86	0	2.1	2	1	1	0	1	3

Tuesday, June 14, 2016

HOME RUN DERBY

José Fernández just doesn't want to pitch in the All-Star Game when it's played in San Diego on July 12.

He wants to participate in the Home Run Derby, as well.

"I want in for sure," Fernández said. "Oh, my God, it would be amazing."

A few pitchers – the Giants' Madison Bumgarner, the Cubs' Jake Arrieta and the Cardinals' Adam Wainwright – have come out within the past week saying they would like to take part in the Derby.

There's no plan in place at the moment to include pitchers in the July 11 Home Run Derby, which features baseball's top sluggers.

But Fernández and some others are all for including pitchers in some variation of the contest.

"We should do our own Home Run Derby," Fernández said of a pitchers-only contest. "I think it would be very fun for baseball. I think the fans would love to see that."

Fernández has two career homers and possesses the most pop on the Marlins' pitching staff.

"He definitely has power," said Marlins catching coach Brian Schneider, who throws batting practice to the team's pitchers. "There's no doubt about it. He hits balls a long way. If he goes and he does do it, he's got a lot of pop, and I would put anything past him."

Said Marlins pitcher Tom Koehler: "I've seen him hit some moon-shot home runs in batting practice, so there's no doubt I think he'd do a good job."

But Schneider said he would also be concerned about a pitcher sustaining an injury in a power-hitting contest simply by swinging too hard.

Koehler, though, doesn't think there would be a high risk for injury. He said daily batting practice for pitchers typically involves a heavy emphasis on bunting, followed by a home run contest.

"Honestly, most of the time, that's all we're doing, is basically a home run derby every day when we take batting practice," Koehler said. "Well, it's bunting, and we swing as hard as we can. So I don't think there's an injury risk necessarily."

Koehler said Fernández is by far the home run king among Marlins pitchers.

"It's not close," Koehler said. "It's kind of the rest of us play amongst ourselves, and he doesn't count."

Marlins slugger Giancarlo Stanton said he wouldn't bet against Fernández in a pitchers-only home run contest.

"Yeah, he could hold his own, for sure," Stanton said. "I've only seen Bumgarner hit aside from him, and I think they'd be on top, from what I've seen."

But Fernández is champing at the bit to go blow-to-blow against fellow hurlers.

"I'm down. I'm ready," Fernández said Monday at Petco Park, where the Marlins were preparing to open a three-game series against the Padres. "And I can practice today, too."

Clark Spencer

Tuesday, July 12, 2016

FACING DAVID ORTIZ

José Fernández will never forget Tuesday night.

And it had nothing to do with his final pitching line.

Instead, Fernández will cherish the moment he became the last pitcher to face David Ortiz in an All-Star Game won by the American League, 4-2.

"It's hard to put it into words when you see him so close," said Fernández, who has been a fan of Ortiz since he was a seventh-grader playing baseball in Cuba. "It was an amazing experience for me."

Fernández had said before the game he'd likely throw very hittable fastballs to Ortiz to see if the retiring superstar would hit one out of Petco Park.

His first offering was clocked at only 80 mph.

"It was a fastball, not a changeup like [Ortiz] said," Fernández said. "I was throwing fastball, fastball, fastball. I threw him a breaking ball and he took it."

That pitch got away from Fernández and nearly hit Ortiz, who playfully opened his arms wide and pointed at him as they each shared a laugh from afar.

"I wanted to hit a home run during that at-bat," Ortiz said. "My boy [Fernández] threw me a changeup instead. I looked at him and I was like, 'What happened?'"

Ortiz walked up the line and, after being replaced by a pinch runner, proceeded to hug his American League teammates.

Fernández tipped his cap from the mound while Ortiz received a standing ovation from the crowd of 42,386.

"I was nervous because I couldn't believe I was actually pitching to him," Fernández said. "It was just great. He signed the jersey that I brought for him. His was the first baseball jersey that I bought when I came to the United States. It was a humbling experience seeing how time really flies by."

Fernández's moment was another highlight in what was one of the most memorable All-Star Game experiences for the Marlins ever.

Fernández, Marcell Ozuna, A.J. Ramos and Fernando Rodney represented the largest Marlins' contingent at the All-Star Game since 2005 and matched a club record.

That followed Giancarlo Stanton's spectacular and record-setting victory in Monday's Home Run Derby when he spread 61 home run balls around Petco Park.

Fernández gave up a run on two hits in 1 1/3 innings with the walk to Ortiz and a strikeout he picked up when he entered in relief of starter Johnny Cueto in the bottom of the second inning.

Cueto gave up home runs to a pair of Royals in that inning — Eric Hosmer and Salvador Perez.

Hosmer, a Cooper City native and graduate of nearby Plantation American Heritage School, was named the Most Valuable Player after finishing two for three with that homer and two RBI.

"It's a great feeling," said Hosmer, who was part of a national championship team in high school at Heritage in 2008. "It's extremely humbling. I never thought about becoming the MVP. I just wanted to soak up the whole experience, and it's everything and more you could ever ask for."

Ozuna went one for two and hit a single that drove in a run in the fourth inning in his first All-Star Game appearance. Ozuna, the first Marlins All-Star starter as an outfielder, became only the first Marlin to record an RBI in the game since Miguel Cabrera in 2005 and only the fourth ever.

"It was awesome for me being a first-time All-Star, and I was ready to play and have fun," Ozuna said. "I'm going to remember everything from being here. You don't get to come here every year and be in this show."

Ozuna came close to hitting a solo home run in the second inning. Ozuna ripped a curveball from Corey Kluber down the left field line that hit the fence just a few feet foul.

Three pitches later, Kluber struck Ozuna out looking on a 94 mph sinker that was the seventh pitch of the at-bat.

Ozuna's single off the Blue Jays' Aaron Sanchez cut the NL's deficit to 4-2.

Ramos, who was also selected to his first All-Star Game, did not pitch.

Rodney struck out Cabrera and induced Michael Saunders to pop out during his relief appearance in the eighth inning. As he walked off the field, Rodney stopped and did his signature crossbow gesture for the fans of his previous ball club. Rodney was traded from the Padres to the Marlins on June 30.

"Being back in San Diego was important for me and something I won't forget because these fans appreciated me," Rodney said. "I gave them the [arrow] to show them that I love them a lot."

Andre C. Fernandez

LAST WEEKS OF THE SEASON

José Fernández pitches in the first inning of the Marlins-Royals game, August 24, 2016. (Pedro Portal/Miami Herald)

Thursday, August 18, 2016

STRIKEOUT KING

José Fernández is on a strikeout binge of historical note.

Fernández, who returns to the mound on Thursday night after receiving a mini midseason vacation, is on pace to finish with one of the highest strikeout rates in major-league history.

And get this: "I'm not even trying to strike people out," Fernández said.

You wouldn't know it from his numbers.

Fernández is averaging 12.94 strikeouts per nine innings.

If he maintains that figure, he will finish with the third-highest strikeout rate in big-league history among starting pitchers with at least 125 innings.

Only Randy Johnson in 2001 (13.41 K/9) and Pedro Martinez in 1999 (13.20) struck out hitters with greater frequency. Both pitchers are in the Hall of Fame.

Fernández needs two more strikeouts to reach 200 for the season and 12 more to break Ryan Dempster's single-season team record of 209, which was set in 2000.

"He's going to hit a lot of milestones for the Marlins," Manager Don Mattingly said. "The longer he's here, he's going to keep hitting milestones."

Fernández said that when he first reached the majors, strikeouts were big to him.

"I was just trying to prove to everybody that I could strike people out, including myself," Fernández said.

But that's no longer the case. Just the opposite.

In what is his first full season since undergoing Tommy John surgery in 2014, Fernández and the Marlins are trying to nurse him along so that he can last the entire season.

Twice they've skipped his turn in the rotation.

Numerous times they've lifted him from starts when his pitch counts begin to climb.

Constantly they've told him to pitch to contact in order to record quick outs and conserve his pitch counts.

"I'm trying to get quick outs so I can get back to the dugout and use less pitches," he said.

"I'm trying to get early contact and get people out quick. I've got to prove to everybody that I can get people out on two or three pitches."

With that goal in mind, Fernández has made greater use of his changeup.

"It's fine to strike people out," Fernández said. "Don't get me wrong. But for some reason, I think I'm mixing [pitches] better, and I have a better game plan."

And the strikeouts are coming at an even greater rate, as a result.

Clark Spencer

Friday, September 9, 2016

CLASH OF TITANS

As one of the few men who has played behind both José Fernández and Clayton Kershaw, utility infielder Miguel Rojas of the Marlins tells people there are no two better pitchers.

"I've told everybody," Rojas said, "they are the best lefty in the game and the best righty."

Kershaw and Fernández.

At Marlins Park on Friday night, the two aces – Kershaw of the Dodgers and Fernández of the Marlins – will square off for the first time in a marquee matchup that has blockbuster written all over it.

José Fernández, pitches in the second inning of the Marlins-Dodgers game, September 9, 2016. (Pedro Portal/el Nuevo Herald)

"I was hoping that this was going to be the wild-card matchup, that's what I was hoping for," ESPN baseball analyst Jim Bowden said. "That would have been a tremendous matchup."

It still is, but under circumstances that diminish some of the luster.

The reeling Marlins are gasping for life in the wild-card race, hooked up to a respirator with an extremely poor prognosis. Their only prayer is a miracle.

The first-place Dodgers, meanwhile, have taken command in the National League West, and they've made their second-half charge without Kershaw, who has spent the past nine weeks on the disabled list with a herniated disk.

This will be his first outing since June 26. As a result, he is not expected to pitch more than four or five innings as the Dodgers ratchet him up for the playoffs.

Clayton Kershaw, pitches in the second inning of the Marlins-Dodgers game, September 9, 2016. (Pedro Portal/el Nuevo Herald)

But even a taste of wine is better than no sip at all.

One Major League scout, who spoke under condition of anonymity, said there's only one other pitching matchup he'd rather see.

"I'd like to see Kershaw against Kershaw," the scout said. "I'd like to see Clayton Kershaw of 2015 face Kershaw of 2016 and see which guy would win. That would be the best matchup because there's nobody in his class right now."

Over the past five years, Kershaw won the Cy Young Award as the National League's best pitcher three times, with one second and one third-place finish. With an 11-2 record and 1.79 ERA, he was angling toward another Cy Young until injury stalled the attempt.

"Clayton Kershaw is still in his prime, and he has been for six straight years," the scout said. "That's amazing."

Then there is the brash Fernández, who is four years Kershaw's junior and lacks his full body of work. Fernández, 24, has won 90 fewer games than Kershaw, 28, and has yet to throw a complete game. Kershaw has thrown three shutouts this season alone and 15 in his career.

But few deny that Fernández's "stuff" is on par with Kershaw's.

"It's the most electric stuff – more electric than Kershaw at certain times," the scout said. "Kershaw just has more experience and a better game-day selection of pitches than José does at this point, and that comes with experience."

Fernández said he admires Kershaw.

"Probably one of the best in the game," Fernández said. "There's no question about that."

But when asked what one pitch of his that he would trade for one of Kershaw's, Fernández refused to yield. He wouldn't trade a thing in terms of the pitches each brings to the table.

"I'm very satisfied with my stuff," Fernández said.

Fernández is averaging 12.57 strikeouts per nine innings this season, a staggering rate that, if it were to continue, would rank as the fourth-best strikeout-per-nine-innings ratio in big-league history. Among starting pitchers, only Randy Johnson (13.41 in 2001), Pedro Martinez (13.20 in 1999) and Kerry Wood (12.58 in 1998) rank higher.

Then there is Fernández's close-to-invincible record at Marlins Park, where he has gone 27-2 with a 1.57 ERA over his career.

"José's my second-favorite pitcher in baseball, period," the scout said. "I would pay to see José Fernández pitch every one of his starts. He might strike out 15 and hit a homer. He does not like to lose. He roots for his teammates as hard as anybody I've ever seen."

Beyond the black-and-white statistics, Rojas said Kershaw and Fernández are similar in ways that fans might not notice. Hitters, when they make contact, are less likely to put the barrel on the ball when the two are pitching.

José Fernández singles in the second inning of the Marlins-Dodgers game, September 9, 2016. (Pedro Portal/el Nuevo Herald)

"When I play shortstop, I see a lot of balls that are hit hard to me," said Rojas, who was with the Dodgers in 2014 before being traded to the Marlins. "But when those guys pitch, the ground balls are softer. Their offspeed pitches are so incredible. For me, it's a blessing to play behind Kershaw and Fernández."

Fernández vs. Kershaw on Friday might lack the high drama of a one-game, winner-take-all wild-card playoff showdown that Bowden was imagining a month ago.

José Fernández, gestures to the stands as he celebrates a 4-1 victory over the Los Angeles Dodgers at Marlins Park, September 9, 2016. (Pedro Portal/el Nuevo Herald)

But there are far worse ways to spend a Friday.

"Unfortunately, this particular matchup isn't what we all wanted to see," Bowden said of a postseason clash between the two. "But I think for the first four innings, it's going to be fun."

Clark Spencer

Tuesday, September 20, 2016

JOSÉ'S FINAL GAME

José Fernández may have pitched his final innings of 2016 on Tuesday night.

If so, Fernández put a nice exclamation point on his best season as a major leaguer.

Fernández struck out 12 batters — at one point retiring 21 Nationals in a row — to help the Marlins beat Washington 1-0.

José Fernández pitches in the second inning of the Miami Marlins vs Washington Nationals game, September 20, 2016. (Pedro Portal/el Nuevo Herald)

The Marlins (75-74) moved over the .500 mark for the first time since Sept. 2, won their third in a row and moved to within four games of the Mets in the Wild Card race.

"I was just trying to get quick outs and follow the game plan," Fernández said. "With the lineup they [the Nationals] have they can do some damage."

Giancarlo Stanton gave Fernández all the run support he would need with a solo home run to right field in the bottom of the sixth inning. The opposite field blast was Stanton's second in two games and his 27th of the season.

"Getting a few at-bats instead of one at-bat a day helps," Stanton said. "That one was just a good swing and a good contact type ball."

Fernández, who did not walk a batter, threw 111 pitches and improved to 16-8, adding to a career-high win total for a season, and lowered his ERA to 2.86.

Fernández entered his second season following Tommy John surgery with a plan to pitch in the neighborhood of 180-190 innings.

José Fernández in the dugout during the first inning, September 20, 2016. (Pedro Portal/Miami Herald)

Fernández's eight shutout frames Tuesday night was his longest start since April 29, 2014 — prior to his injury — and brought his total for the season to 182 2/3 innings.

Should Fernández make his next start it would be Sunday at home against the Braves.

"I'm not the manager," Fernández said. "I'll come in here tomorrow and I'll cheer my teammates and I'll be ready to go if I have to go and I understand that whatever happens, it's not my call."

Fernández continued to thrive both at home and against the Nationals (88-63), who lost their fourth in a row.

Fernández improved to 29-2 in 42 career starts at Marlins Park with a 1.49 ERA, and improved to 7-0 with a 0.99 ERA in 10 career starts against Washington.

It was Fernández's eighth start this season without allowing a run, his ninth double-digit strikeout game, and the Marlins recorded their third shutout when he starts.

José Fernández and second baseman Dee Gordon celebrate 1-0 victory, September 20, 2016. (Pedro Portal/Miami Herald)

Fernández's 21 consecutive batters retired was a career-best streak and the third-longest in Marlins' history tying Ricky Nolasco (Aug. 18, 2008 in San Francisco) and two behind the club record of 23 in a row shared by Nolasco and Kevin Brown.

"I feel like it was the best game José's thrown all year," Marlins Manager Don Mattingly said. "He used his changeup early in the game. That was a weapon for him all game, keeping them off balance. I thought he was calm today. He wasn't over-throwing. He showed a lot of really good things today."

After giving up a double to Stephen Drew, the second batter he faced, Fernández did not allow another base runner until Wilson Ramos hit a bloop single to center field in the eighth. That was followed by a high-chopper that found its way into right field off the bat of Brian Goodwin.

Fernández, who had thrown 103 pitches to that point, struck out Danny Espinosa and induced a ground out to second from pinch hitter Daniel Murphy to preserve the lead.

"I think it's all the process of learning how to pitch and trying to make a pitch and not overthrow it," Fernández said. "Not try to make it unhittable and just try to put it where they can't do so much damage and get a ground ball."

With closer A.J. Ramos unavailable after pitching in four of the past five games, David Phelps picked up his fourth save.

In the ninth inning, Phelps took a grounder off the bat of Drew off his right leg resulting in a single. Phelps stayed in the game, struck out Bryce Harper and induced Anthony Rendon to ground into a fielder's choice to end the game.

"I knew it hit me in the meat," Phelps said. "The bigger panic for me was figuring out where the ball was to try and get the out. We'll see how it feels tomorrow."

Stanton played six innings and got a chance to test himself physically as he continues his return from a severe groin strain. Stanton jumped for Drew's double in the first inning coming up just short near the wall.

José Fernández interviewed by Fox Sports Florida's Jessica Blaylock after the game, September 20, 2016. (Pedro Portal/el Nuevo Herald)

"I felt pretty good out there," Stanton said. "This is as interesting as it gets. One day it will be really tight like I can't move and the other day it will be like nothing is wrong. I was interested to see how it would react after that jump and it felt fine."

Andre C. Fernandez

Chapter 10

A REMARKABLE JOURNEY

MILESTONES

BORN
July 31, 1992, Santa Clara, Villa Clara, Cuba.

HIGH SCHOOL
Braulio Alonso (Tampa)

PURSUED BY
Cincinnati Reds. Ruled ineligible (eligibility exhausted) by the FHSAA before his senior year in 2011, the Reds attempt to sign Fernandez as an international free agent. Fernandez wins an FHSAA appeal, ending Cincinnati's pursuit.

DRAFTED
Florida Marlins in the 1st round (14th pick) of the 2011 amateur draft.

SIGNED
August 15, 2011 ($2 million bonus)

MINOR LEAGUES
2011: Gulf Coast League Marlins; Jamestown (New York-Penn League). 2012: Greensboro (South Atlantic League), Jupiter (Florida State League). 2015: Jupiter (FSL, injury rehab); Jacksonville (Southern League, injury rehab)

MLB DEBUT
April 7, 2013.

AWARDS
2013 NL Rookie of the Year (third place in 2013 Cy Young voting)

MONTHLY AWARDS
NL Rookie of the Month, July, 2013; NL Rookie of the Month, August, 2013; NL Pitcher of the Month, April, 2014.

WEEKLY AWARDS
NL Player of the Week, July 28, 2013; NL Player of the Week, Aug. 25, 2013; NL Player of the Week, April 6, 2014; NL Player of the Week, May 15, 2016.

Thursday, September 29, 2016

JOSÉ FERNÁNDEZ (1992-2016)

When he was not throwing heat from the pitcher's mound or pulling pranks on teammates in the dugout or playing dominoes with his grandmother, José Fernández could often be found on a boat.

The ocean represented freedom to Fernández, who had fled Fidel Castro's island dictatorship in Cuba to pursue his American baseball dream in Florida. The Miami Marlins ace lived and played with a joyousness that embodied the gratitude he felt for the opportunities stretching out before him on the infinite blue horizon.

Fernández was as competitive on the water as he was on the diamond. His favorite catch was swordfish, a fighting fish, just like the marlin.

José Fernández shows off a prize dolphin catch, undated. (José Fernández/Instagram)

His remarkable journey began and ended on a boat. He survived the treacherous crossing of what Cubans call the "Caribbean's largest cemetery," jumping in to rescue his mother from drowning one stormy night. He died when his 32-foot SeaVee named *Kaught Looking* crashed at high speed into the South Pointe jetty at 3:15 a.m. Sunday, killing Fernández and two friends. A day later, four baseballs autographed by him washed up on the beach.

Fernández was 24. He is survived by his mother, grandmother, stepfather, stepsister and a girlfriend who is expecting Fernández's first child, a baby daughter, in February.

"So many times we talked about dreams, things left to do, the future," said Ramon Jimenez, the stepdad who raised Fernández from infancy. "He was the light of everyone and now that light has been extinguished."

Fernández was excited about becoming a father. The 2013 National League Rookie of the Year could also look forward to more All-Star games, future Cy Young awards, and a huge payday after his initial contract expired in 2018. His 100-mph fastball was feared, his slider so elusive it was nicknamed "The Defector." He burned with a fire to win and he'd remind the manager, "Hey, I'm available to hit!" even on his off days. Fernández, who threw a team-record 253 strikeouts while earning $2.8 million this season, might have commanded up to $30 million per year, although probably not with the frugal Marlins.

"He was like a little kid," Manager Don Mattingly said, describing Fernández's energy.

Fernández spent his last night on his boat, hoping to blow off steam about something that was bothering him, possibly a spat with his girlfriend. He invited his best friend on the team, Marcell Ozuna – whom he had nicknamed Oso, Bear – to come along.

"I told him, 'Don't go out,' but everybody knew he was crazy about that boat," Ozuna said. "I didn't think my brother would be gone so soon. It's left an empty feeling so big."

José Fernández with his father Ramon Jimenez, undated. (el Nuevo Herald)

Fernández, who docked his boat at the Cocoplum Yacht Club, wound up at the American Social bar and restaurant on the Miami

River with friend Eddy Rivero, who phoned his friend Emilio Macias to join them. The two young men who grew up in West Kendall went for a spin along South Beach with Fernández, even though another friend warned them not to go boating so late at night. Miami-Dade Fire Rescue divers found two bodies trapped beneath the boat, which was upended on the jetty rocks, and one body on the ocean floor.

"I want to erase from my mind the images of the accident," Jimenez said. "I want to remember José as that good boy, full of life, who fought like a lion on the field and gave me the most tender hugs."

Fernández was scheduled to make his last start of his season on Monday. Instead, he was honored by tearful teammates who wore No. 16 Fernández jerseys during their victory over the New York Mets. He was remembered by Miami on Wednesday when people waved goodbye as the hearse carrying Fernández's casket drove from Marlins Park through Little Havana where he'd once been Grand Marshal of the Three Kings Parade to the seaside Shrine of Our Lady of Charity, the patron saint of Cuba, a monument to Cuban exiles. Later, thousands paid their respects at a viewing at St. Brendan Catholic Church.

"It was easy to love José," said Dan Jennings, former Marlins assistant general manager and manager who treated Fernández like a son. "He was like a big puppy, and when he walked in the room everyone wanted to pet him. He had that infectious smile that speaks all languages. He was a perfect match for Miami."

Fernández grew up in Santa Clara on a small farm with his mother, Maritza, and stepfather. He shared a bedroom with his grandmother. He used to go door to door selling tomatoes and onions.

From a young age, he was fascinated with Cuba's national pastime, *beisbol*. He'd wander the fields searching for the perfect stick and collecting rocks, then practice hitting home runs by himself.

He formulated a vision of himself as a pitcher with a fastball that would turn batters into pretzels. His grandmother, a knowledgeable fan, used to catch for him in the yard, giving him pointers on his delivery.

He attended the provincial sports school and played for junior national teams.

Marlins Manager Dan Jennings, May 23, 2015. (Pedro Portal/el Nuevo Herald)

Jimenez, feeling stymied in his career as a doctor, tried 13 times to leave Cuba, but each time a snitch in the group waiting on the beach for the boat would alert the authorities and the plan was aborted. Jimenez finally got to Florida on his 14th try in 2005 and settled in Tampa, where he found a job at a car wash and then at a hospital and sent money to his family so they could arrange to pay smugglers.

Fernández, then 14, tried to leave the island three times, once getting close enough to see the lights of Miami before the U.S. Coast Guard returned him and his fellow passengers to Cuba. As punishment, he was sent to prison for two months, where he said he shared cell space with a mass murderer.

On his fourth try, 15-year-old Fernández, his mother, his step-sister, her mother and eight others departed from Trinidad, on the south coast, following the longer, less-patrolled route to Cancun, Mexico.

They encountered rough seas and everyone was retching over the side. When Fernández heard a splash and screams, he jumped in and swam through towering waves to rescue a woman he did not know was his mother until he reached her and told her to climb on his back.

National League Rookie of the Year, José Fernández, was honored as the Grand Marshal of the 2014 Three Kings Day Parade, January 12, 2014. (Hector Gabino/el Nuevo Herald)

Once they reached shore in Mexico, they took two bus rides to the Texas border, getting robbed along the way. They stepped onto American soil on April 5, 2008. They joined Jimenez in Tampa.

That's when Fernández met the man who molded him into a major-league prospect. Orlando Chinea, former pitching coach for the Cuban national team, mentor to Rolando Arrojo, José Contreras, Livan Hernandez and Orlando "El Duque" Hernandez, had defected to Tampa in 2004. Chinea took *"el niño"* under his wing.

"He could throw the ball 82 mph, but he couldn't pitch," Chinea recalled. "Everyone has a talent – singers, writers, dancers. But you need the right person to develop it. If José had stayed in Cuba, he would have stayed mediocre."

That summer, Hernandez trained nearly every day from 8 a.m. to 1:30 p.m. with his gruff teacher, who employed such old-school workout methods as flipping truck tires, tossing medicine balls, running in sand and chopping down trees in the woods. He also ordered 90-minute stretching sessions.

"We built the strength that gave him his power," Chinea said. "We developed his mechanics and his command. He learned quick because he was smart. He had a strong personality, like me."

At Tampa Alonso High School, pitching coach Pete Toledo, also a Cuban immigrant, helped Fernández adjust to American culture and practice his English. Toledo knew the kid from Cuba who had no baseball gear was special the first day of fall tryouts when instead of filling out his evaluation sheet with the usual grades, "I drew a big fat line through the whole row of categories and a huge star next to his name and wrote, 'We're going to Omaha!' " Toledo said, using an expression that refers to the College World Series.

Fernández played like he had in Cuba, where showmanship is not frowned upon. He'd argue with umpires, yell *"¡Sientate!"* (sit down) after strikeouts, raise his fists jubilantly when he hit a home run.

Orlando Chinea, left, and Alfonso Urquiola, Tokyo 1995. (Miami Herald)

"He arrived here with that Latin flavor, very passionate and emotional on the field," Toledo said. "My job was to rein him in and tone him down. The kids loved him. He made everyone better because they all wanted to work as hard as he did."

Fernández trained with Chinea in the evenings. After a 14-strikeout game he received praise from his coaches, but Chinea told him he pitched "like a kindergartner throwing with a short arm." Fernández got angry and stomped away. Chinea suspended him for two weeks for acting "spoiled."

"I told him we're working to be great in the major leagues, not in high school," Chinea said. "Our goal was for José to become the second Cuban-born player to win the Cy Young Award after Mike Cuellar. All three of us were from Santa Clara."

Fernández raised homing pigeons as a hobby. On the team trip to Alonso's 2009 state championship, the bus pulled over in Bartow for a bathroom stop and Fernández brought out a box with two pigeons. He gave one to head coach Landy Faedo, who questioned whether the birds would find their way back to Tampa.

"I know mine will but yours might get lost or eaten by a hawk," Fernández said, laughing.

When they returned to Tampa, Fernández's pigeon was home, but Faedo's never showed up.

"It's a story we still remember," Toledo said. "The kid was fun."

Fernández wrote "99" on the locker room mirror, signifying the fastball velocity he wanted to attain; the number is faded but still there five years after Fernández led Alonso to the second of two state titles he won.

After the season, Fernández continued to work long hours with Chinea, whom he nicknamed "Mr. Miyagi," after the master in the "Karate Kid" movies. Chinea called Fernández by the name his relatives used, his middle name, Delfin.

"For me, he was my Delfi, my big boy," Chinea said, his voice cracking. "No one loved baseball more than Delfi. No one. I'm going to miss him."

Fernández, 18, was picked No. 14 by the Marlins in the 2011 draft. He spent his first and only minor league season dominating at Single A Greensboro, North Carolina.

"The talent was good, the competitive fire is what set him apart," said his manager, Dave Berg. "Even on his off days when he was charting pitches from the stands and we'd be losing, he'd get mad.

"He was happy-go-lucky but driven to be the best. After he pitched he'd come into the office and ask questions: 'What else do you got for me? Where can I improve?' "

Fernández was called up unexpectedly soon for the start of the 2013 season when three Marlins pitchers got injured. He was just what the franchise needed after a disappointing first season in the new ballpark. He finished 12-6 with a 2.19 ERA, made the All-Star team and was named NL Rookie of the Year.

Life was grand, except he longed to see his *abuela*, "the love of his life," Olga Fernández, the grandmother who was back in Cuba, listening to his games on the radio from the roof of her house, the only place she could get reception. He sent her gifts, they talked and cried on the phone, she gave him updates on the Cuban league, critiques of his pitching performances and scouting reports. Separated by that ocean, they had not seen each other in five years.

"Whenever I asked about his father, he changed the subject," Jennings said. "But when we talked about his grandmother, he got emotional. He revered her. He was devoted to her and his mother."

In November, after lengthy negotiation with the Cuban government by Jennings and Marlins owner Jeffrey Loria, Olga Fernández obtained a visa and flew to Miami.

"We fooled José by telling him to come to the clubhouse for an interview," Jennings said. "When his grandmother walked through that door, he was paralyzed with happiness. It was one of the most heartwarming reunions you can imagine. He hugged her, walked her out to the field, showed her the mound, pointed to the seats where she would sit to watch him pitch. I realized then how genuine he was, how loving he was."

Fernández's 2014 season was cut short by an elbow injury and Tommy John surgery. He spent months in rehab in Coconut Grove with therapist Ron Yacoub. He ran up and down the Rickenbacker Causeway bridge.

José Fernández with his grandmother, Olga Fernández, undated. (el Nuevo Herald)

"I'd go visit him at 8 a.m. and there he was, attacking rehab the same way he would an opponent," Jennings said. "That was a lonely time. I've never seen any player work harder."

Fernández became a U.S. citizen in April 2015 and resumed playing July 2.

Super fan Andres Salgado "The José Guy," having a haircut by José Fernández, as the official barber of the Marlins Hugo "Juice" Tandron, left smiles before game against the San Francisco Giants at Marlin Park. Salgado spent 13-plus months growing his hair in honor of Fernández's return from Tommy John surgery, July 1, 2015. (David Santiago/el Nuevo Herald)

"When it was his turn to bat, he stood on the steps and said, 'Hey, Papi, DJ, I'm going to hit a home run for my grandmother,'" Jennings said. "And he did! She was in the front row. Wow. It was like a Disney movie."

Fernández was proud of his hitting ability. When he was in the batting cage, he insisted that coaches and teammates gather to watch. One time, when he hit a home run against Atlanta, and admired his handiwork a little too blatantly, he went into the Braves' clubhouse afterward to apologize for letting his Cuban brashness burst forth.

"He liked to needle people, he was a jokester, but he also made fun of himself," Jennings said. "If he made a mistake, he owned up to it. He was a unifier. People gravitated toward him."

Fernández looked better than ever in 2016, when he made the All-Star team and went 16-8, pitching eight shutout innings and striking out 12 in a 1-0 win over the Washington Nationals in his last start.

"I texted him: Cut that crap out, we're trying to win the division," said Jennings, now with the Nationals.

In his spare time, Fernández liked relaxing at the big house in west Miami-Dade that he bought for his family for $680,000 two years ago. He was an unabashed mama's boy.

He was enjoying his new life with Maria Arias, sister-in-law of his friend, Jessie Garcia, a professional fisherman. He and former Marlins cheerleader Carla Mendoza had broken off their engagement five months ago. Mendoza posted a tribute to Fernández on her Instagram account: "My deepest love goes out to those who saw José as more than an athlete, but as a passionate, raw human being. I'm fortunate enough to have loved and be loved by José and his family for over 3 crazy, beautiful years."

He liked to eat at Havana Harry's, play pool or sing karaoke at the Sunset Tavern, party in Miami Beach. Some people close to him were worried that he was having too much fun for his own good.

"I think the Marlins should have given him a personal adviser to help take care of his behavior outside the baseball field," Chinea said.

José Fernández hugs his girlfriend Carla Mendoza after defeating the Atlanta Braves 12-11 and becoming the first pitcher in the modern era to win his first 17 career home decisions, September 25, 2015. (David Santiago/el Nuevo Herald)

Most of all, Fernández was drawn to the ocean. He fished avidly with friends and in tournaments with J's Crew, Garcia's fishing team. A few weeks before his death, an Instagram video shows Fernández reeling in a fish and dancing with bikini-clad women. He'd bombard Jennings with photos of himself, tan and smiling, prize catches hanging from each hand, gleaming in the sun.

Fernández liked to ride across the waves to the Bahamas to fish for swordfish, wahoo, grouper. Sometimes he'd drive his boat from Miami to Cat Cay for lunch.

"When he had extra time he would play basketball with the club members' kids," said assistant dockmaster Bernard Shepherd. "He was very, very nice, very generous."

Summer campers from the Kiwanis of Little Havana meet José Fernández during a field trip to the Miami Children's Museum on Watson Island, July 9, 2013. (Daniel Bock/el Nuevo Herald)

Fernández lived the way he pitched. His wrecked boat has been impounded by authorities. The ocean that was his path to freedom, his sanctuary, became his grave, and the city captivated by his story tries to comprehend its ending.

Linda Robertson, Michelle Kaufman

JOSÉ FERNÁNDEZ
CAREER STATISTICS

YEAR	W	L	ERA	GP	GS	SV	IP	H	R	ER	HR	BB	SO
2013	12	6	2.19	28	28	0	172.2	111	47	42	10	58	187
2014	4	2	2.44	8	8	0	51.2	36	19	14	4	13	70
2015	6	1	2.92	11	11	0	64.2	61	21	21	4	14	79
2016	16	8	2.86	29	29	0	182.1	149	63	58	13	55	253
Totals	38	17	2.58	76	76	0	471.1	357	150	135	31	140	589

Monday, October 3, 2016

A HUGE VOID

Had Sunday been a must-win for the Marlins, José Fernández would have been on the mound for them. But Fernández died tragically, the Marlins were playing for nothing and their season came to a merciful end.

All Sunday's 10-7 loss did was allow an emotionally drained team to dash home for the winter and try to process what has been a week-long nightmare that began with the death of its star pitcher in a boating crash.

"Obviously, the circumstances just dramatically changed the final thoughts on the season," Manager Don Mattingly said in what was his final sit-down dugout session with reporters before Sunday's game.

To say the least.

The Marlins failed to make the postseason for the 13th consecutive season. They finished below .500 (79-82) for the seventh year in a row.

And now they begin the task of moving forward without the one player they could least afford to lose. Mattingly will return to Miami to chart out an uncertain future with front-office executives, one that does not involve Fernández.

That process starts Monday.

"What's happened in the last few days puts a big question mark on that," Mattingly said. "Obviously, José was a huge piece of what we're doing. He's your ace. He's your guy. It's not the time to think about it or talk about it, but it won't be long [before] we'll have to."

The first steps will be minor ones. Within the coming few days, the Marlins are expected to decide on their coaching staff, where one or two changes could be made.

Then comes the heavy lifting.

The Marlins must decide not only how to address the huge void left by Fernández, but any other roster questions that need to be examined. For example, would the Marlins now field trade offers on Giancarlo Stanton or Marcell Ozuna in order to acquire a pitcher?

The free agent market for pitchers is unappealing, and the Marlins don't have the kind of attractive prospects in their farm system they could use to reel in a top-rung pitcher, and certainly not one of Fernández's caliber.

For Mattingly, Sunday was a time to reflect on his first season with the Marlins, who stood at nine games over .500 on July 31 before fading over the final two months.

"When I came into spring training – and without saying it out loud – I knew there were certain things that had to happen [to reach the playoffs], and part of that was we had to be injury-free," Mattingly said.

That didn't happen.

The Marlins were dealt major losses with injuries to Stanton, Justin Bour, Wei-Yin Chen, Adam Conley and A.J. Ramos – all of them coming in the second half.

Mattingly, though optimistic the Marlins had a chance to end their postseason drought, had other concerns.

"I knew we were going to have a young club coming down the stretch," Mattingly said. "How we were going to react to that I wasn't quite sure."

Mattingly echoed a sentiment that is shared by many managers of non-playoff teams this time of year, that next year will be better. Every manager of the Marlins since 2003, the last time they made the playoffs, has said the same thing.

"I realistically thought and felt pretty good about our club having a shot to play in the postseason," Mattingly said. "That didn't happen, but I think this season has a chance to be a steppingstone for us moving forward to next year.

Clark Spencer

AFTERWORD

MARITZA GÓMEZ FERNÁNDEZ, MOTHER OF JOSÉ FERNÁNDEZ

José Fernández is my only child. I shared him with an entire community who also loved him. My pain is profound. I know yours is, too. You loved him like a son, grandson, brother and friend; even those who never met him. You valued him as a baseball star, but regarded him as one among you.

Thanks to this great country that welcomed us, my son achieved his dream of reaching Major League Baseball and becoming a U.S. citizen. He never stopped loving Cuba deeply, but the United States was an inspiration for him.

I've been sustained by your love for my son. As his mother, thank you for that blessing. On behalf of my family, especially my mother, thank you for your prayers for him, Maria, and my granddaughter in her womb. I want to thank the community for supporting us in this, the most difficult moment of our lives. The love we've received helps us cope with this harsh reality.

I want to thank his Marlins family, Jeffrey Loria, David Samson, Michael Hill, his coaches, trainers and teammates over the years. I also want to thank his agent, Scott Boras. The moments he shared with all of you filled him with joy. At the Marlins, his dreams were highlighted and others were reached. It was there where he interacted with fans, offered his smile, and his joy for baseball.

My son was always thinking about how to help others. He had passion for helping children with cancer through *Live Like Bella*. He loved to engage with young people and inspire their future. He shared moments with Sabrina, a young lady with Down syndrome, to bring a smile to her face. He spent time with the older generation to connect with his roots. Amidst this nightmare, I thank God that my son, though young, left a real mark on this community, and you left one on him.

In the most inconsolable moments, in disbelief for what occurred, came the solemn procession on the streets of Miami. Along that difficult route, I saw the love at the ballpark from Marlins players and employees, and the community. I felt strength from the blessing at La Ermita, a sacred place for Cubans. I saw people on the sidewalks; the Cuban coffee salute at La Carreta, where the flags of Cuba and the United States were presented as symbols of my son's patriotism. And, in a deeply profound moment for our family, I witnessed thousands visit St. Brendan's to pay their respects.

Our comfort that night was everyone's expression of love. It gave us strength. I also want to thank the Marlins, local authorities, the Miami-Dade Police and City of Miami Police Departments, St. Brendan's, the clergy, musicians and choir, the media, and all who worked to offer my son a beautiful farewell. I want to thank Caballero Rivero Funeral Home and all who sent flowers and contributions to JDF16 Foundation. I want to thank MLB for all the tributes for my son.

I ask now for your continued prayers and that we all continue to pray for Emilio and Eduardo, and their loved ones. They have also suffered greatly. Please pray for Maria and Penelope.

And, a final request on behalf of my family: Live out the legacy of my son, José Fernández. Laugh like he did. Live joyfully the way he did. And I ask every little and major leaguer alike to enjoy the game the way he did. Let us continue to love Cuba and the United States as he did. Thank you for loving him, not forgetting him, and keeping his legacy alive.

My dearest son, thank you for being the best gift God gave me. Thank you for the kindheartedness you offered the community. Thank you for offering them your smile. I know that from Heaven you see how much everyone appreciated it.

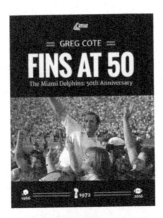